Zionism

Short Histories of Big Ideas Series List

Published

Capitalism By Paul Bowles

Feminism By June Hannam

Environmentalism By David Peterson del Mar

Communism By Mark Sandie

Nationalism By Richard Bosworth

Terrorism By Rosemary O'Kane

Colonialism By Norrie Macqueen

Modernism By Robin Walz

Zionism By David Engel

Available soon

Fascism By Martin Blinkhorn

Zionism

David Engel

PEARSON

Longman

Harlow, England • London • New York • Boston • San Francisco • Toronto
Sydney • Tokyo • Singapore • Hong Kong • Seoul • Taipei • New Delhi
Cape Town • Madrid • Mexico City • Amsterdam • Munich • Paris • Milan

PEARSON EDUCATION LIMITED

Edinburgh Gate
Harlow CM20 2JE
United Kingdom
Tel: +44 (0)1279 623623
Fax: +44 (0)1279 431059
Website: www.pearsoned.co.uk

_____

First edition published in Great Britain in 2009

© Pearson Education Limited 2009

The right of David Engel to be identified as author
of this work has been asserted by him in accordance
with the Copyright, Designs and Patents Act 1988.

ISBN: 978-1-4058-3556-5

British Library Cataloguing in Publication Data
A CIP catalogue record for this book can be obtained from the British Library

Library of Congress Cataloging in Publication Data
A CIP catalog record for this book can be obtained from the Library of
Congress

10 9 8 7 6 5 4 3 2 1
13 12 11 10 09

Set by 35 in 9/15pt Iowan
Printed in Malaysia (CTP-VVP)

The Publisher's policy is to use paper manufactured from sustainable forests.

For Shirley and Harold

Contents

Series editor's preface

WHAT MAKES THE WORLD MOVE? Great men? Irresistible forces? Catastrophic events?

When listening to the morning news on the radio, reading our daily newspapers, following debates on the internet, watching evening television, all of these possibilities – and more – are offered as explanations of the troubles that beset the world in the Middle East, the 'war on terror' in Iraq and Afghanistan, environmental disasters at Chernobyl or New Orleans, and genocide in Sudan or Rwanda.

Where should we look to find answers to the puzzles of the present? To psychology? To economics? To sociology? To political science? To philosophy? Each of these disciplines offer insights into the personalities and the subterranean forces that propel the events that change the world, and within each of these disciplines there are experts who dissect current affairs on the foundation of these insights.

But all of these events, these problems, and even these disciplines themselves have one thing in common: they have a history. And it is through an understanding of the history of those ideas that inspired the people behind the events, and the ideas behind the ideologies that attempted to explain and control the forces around them that we can comprehend the perplexing and confusing world of the present day.

'Short Histories of Big Ideas' aims to provide readers with clear, concise and readable explanations of those ideas that were instrumental in shaping the twentieth century and that continue to shape – and reshape – the present. Everyone who attempts to follow the events of today via newspapers, television, radio and the internet cannot help but see or hear references to 'capitalism', 'communism', 'feminism', 'environmentalism', 'nationalism', 'colonialism' and many other 'isms'. And, while most of us probably believe that we have a basic understanding of what these terms mean, we are probably much less certain about who it was that coined, invented or defined them. Even more murky is our understanding of how these concepts moved from an idea to become an ideology and, perhaps, a phenomenon that changed the world. Most bewildering may be the disputes and controversies between factions and divisions within the movements and political parties that claim to be the true followers and the legitimate heirs of those who first conceived of the concepts to which they claim to adhere.

The authors of these 'Short Histories' have been asked to write accessible, jargon-free prose with the goal of making comprehensible to the intelligent, interested but non-expert reader these highly complicated concepts. In each instance the approach taken is chronological, as each author attempts to explain the origins of these ideas, to describe the people who created them and then to follow the twisting path they followed from conception to the present. Each author in the series is an expert in the field, with a mastery of the literature on the subject – and a desire to convey to readers the knowledge and the understanding that the research of specialist scholars has produced, but which is normally inaccessible to those not engaged in studying these subjects in an academic environment.

The work of specialists often seems remote, obscure, even pedantic, to the non-specialist, but the authors in this series are committed to the goal of bringing the insights and understanding of specialists to a wider public, to concerned citizens and general readers who wish to go beyond today's headlines and form a more comprehensive and meaningful picture of today's world.

Gordon Martel
Series Editor

To the reader

TYPE THE WORD 'ZIONISM' into your favourite internet search engine and you'll generate somewhere between 500,000 and 1,500,000 links. As contemporary 'isms' go, that's not many: it's about the same as you'll find for 'environmentalism' or 'orientalism' but only a quarter of the references to 'liberalism' or 'imperialism', one-fifth of those to 'feminism' or 'socialism', less than one-tenth of those to 'capitalism', and a mere 1.5 or 2 per cent of allusions to 'terrorism'. Still, if you could measure the passion, positive and negative, with which the word is usually mentioned, you'd be tempted to think that Zionism generates more heat than any other political or social movement today. Indeed, neutral descriptions are hard to find. To its many advocates the name suggests a genuinely democratic and progressive movement of national liberation that has given an oppressed and homeless people the freedom, security and dignity denied it for two thousand years. Its opponents, in contrast, claim that in pursuing their aims Zionists have actually created a *new* oppressed and homeless people. Moreover, they charge, the sources of Zionism are the same ones that bred western colonialism and racism, meaning that its ideas must be rejected by all right-thinking human beings.

Perhaps Zionism arouses such strong emotions because for decades it has shaped the lives of millions of people on the most basic and visible existential level. It has brought great good to some, great ill to others. You might ask whether morally the good outweighs the ill or vice versa. In order to answer that question you'd need a moral scale for weighing one person's gain against another's loss. Creating such a scale isn't an easy thing to do. This book won't try to do so. Instead it will show you where the Zionist movement came from, how it formulated its goals and pursued them, how its efforts obtained the results they did, and how its most visible apparent success – the establishment of the State of Israel – has affected its ongoing activities. In other words, this is a history book, not a polemic. You may come away from reading it thinking that Zionism has been an admirable endeavour or an execrable one. You may see its leading figures as heroes or villains. You may find certain aspects of the movement and its history more to your liking or disfavour than others. Whatever you decide, the book has not been written in the hope that you will feel any particular way. Its sole purpose is to help you make sense of some controversies surrounding this contemporary 'ism' and to evaluate the historical arguments of partisans on both sides from an informed perspective.

In that spirit, the book makes a conscious effort to avoid replicating the historical narratives that Zionism's partisans or adversaries have constructed over the years. Those narratives have been produced to legitimize or delegitimize the movement, and they are concerned largely with rebutting the other's claims. As a result they are often loaded with hot-button words, and clashes over them centre about whether one particular term or another corresponds most closely to historical reality. In truth, these arguments have more to do with the meanings people attach to words than with the history they are supposed to describe. Thus the book doesn't concern itself with them. If you hope to find out, say, whether Zionism is or isn't a 'racist' idea, or whether Menachem Begin or Yasir Arafat should be called a 'terrorist' or a 'freedom fighter', you will be disappointed. Making such determinations is a matter of moral judgement; words that express such judgement are beyond the book's pale.

The book is about Zionism, not the State of Israel, Jewish–Arab relations in Palestine or conflict in the Middle East. To be sure, those subjects are closely related to Zionism, but the Zionist movement's history is not identical to theirs. More than anything else, the Zionist movement has spoken to Jews, urging them to behave in certain ways. People who have called themselves Zionists have often disagreed about precisely what behaviour the label implied, and it has not always been clear what united them beyond a common name. The history of Zionism is largely the story of those disagreements – of the situations that produced them, the manner and extent to which they were resolved, and the factors that brought the movement together and permitted it to act despite fairly constant disunity in its ranks. It is also in significant part the story of how different groups of Jews received the Zionists' various messages at different times. Those stories were profoundly influenced by actors beyond the Jewish world, as well as by the government of Israel, whose founding did not obviate the movement's existence. The book thus relates those actors' deeds to the degree that they affected Zionist thought and action. However, it doesn't consider them beyond that point. As a result, you won't find a continuous description of the development of the Palestinian

Arab national movement, British imperial interests in the eastern Mediterranean or the Israeli military, but only snapshots of them when they impinged most directly upon Zionist history.

Because Zionists addressed mainly Jews, the most significant context for understanding what they said and did is Jewish history. The first Zionists were products of that history; it, more than anything else, shaped how they understood the world and brought them together under a common banner. Thus, if you want to know where the Zionist movement came from, you'll need some rudimentary information about what Jews experienced as a group before the movement first appeared on the scene. That's where Chapter 1 begins.

Timeline

721 BCE	Ancient Kingdom of Israel absorbed into Assyrian Empire
586 BCE	Ancient Kingdom of Judah (Judea) becomes province of Babylonian Empire
135 CE	Rome renames province of Judea *Syria Palaestina*
632 CE	Muslim armies conquer Palestine, with 200,000 Jewish residents
1517	Palestine becomes part of Ottoman Empire
1700	Jewish population of Palestine reaches historic low of 3,000
1700–1880	Jews seeking to induce messianic age migrate to Palestine in increasing numbers, raising the country's Jewish population to 24,000
1850s	Improved transportation and communication spur European interest and investment in Palestine; country begins economic upturn
1875–77	Perez Smolenskin publishes articles calling upon Jews to define themselves as a modern 'nation'
1881	Violence against Jews in Russian Empire spurs talk of mass migration; Smolenskin urges Jews to migrate to Palestine as a group

1881–1899   25,000 Jews enter Palestine, constituting First Aliyah

1882   Leo Pinsker's pamphlet, *Autoemancipation*, suggests Jews seek collective political sovereignty; Jewish students from Kharkov establish first modern Jewish agricultural settlement in Palestine

1884   Kattowitz Conference creates Odessa Committee, an umbrella organization for Hibbat Tsiyon societies promoting Jewish agricultural settlement in Palestine

1890   Word 'Zionism' first appears in print

1891   Ahad Ha'am visits Palestine and warns of potential for conflict between Jewish immigrants and native non-Jewish residents

1896   Theodor Herzl publishes *The Jewish State*, suggesting European powers will help Jews obtain sovereignty over an extra-European territory, and begins abortive negotiations with Ottoman Empire to set Palestine aside as a territory for Jews

1897   First World Zionist Congress convenes in Basel; Zionist Organization (ZO) established

1898   Herzl meets Kaiser Wilhelm II in unsuccessful effort to obtain German backing for Zionist programme; Jewish Colonial Bank established as ZO's chief financial instrument

1901   Herzl granted audience with Sultan but fails to gain Ottoman sanction for Zionist project; Democratic Fraction formed in opposition to Herzl's leadership of ZO; ZO establishes Jewish National Fund to purchase land for Jewish settlement in Palestine

1903	Britain proposes to sponsor Jewish settlement in East Africa, prompting heated debate at Sixth Zionist Congress; Mizrahi (religious Zionist) party founded
1903–1914	Second Aliyah brings 32,500 Jews to Palestine
1904	Herzl dies in midst of East Africa controversy
1905	Seventh Zionist Congress rejects East Africa proposal
1907	ZO establishes office in Palestine
1908	Young Turk Revolution
1909	First kibbutz established at Degania; Tel Aviv founded
1911	Arthur Ruppin commits ZO to principle of Hebrew labour
1915	Sir Henry McMahon tells Hussein ibn Ali that Britain will support Arab independence in Ottoman Middle East in return for Arab military action against Ottoman forces
1916	Sykes–Picot Agreement envisions British–French partition of Ottoman Middle East
1917	Balfour Declaration expresses British favour for 'national home for the Jewish people in Palestine'
1917–1918	British military forces expel Ottomans from Palestine and begin military occupation of country
1918–1919	Pogroms in Eastern Europe claim lives of 60,000 Jews
1919	General Syrian Congress demands Arab control of entire Ottoman Middle East
1919–1923	Third Aliyah brings 35,000 Jews to Palestine
1920	San Remo Conference awards Britain mandate to govern Palestine; Herbert Samuel becomes first

	high commissioner; Histadrut labour federation and Haganah guard force established
1921	Colonial Secretary Winston Churchill severs Transjordan from area designated for Jewish National Home
1922	League of Nations ratifies British mandate for Palestine; Churchill White Paper gives first official interpretation of 'Jewish National Home'
1923	Pinhas Rutenberg establishes Palestine Electric Corporation, spurring private investment in Jewish Palestine
1924–1926	Fourth Aliyah brings 60,000 Jews to Palestine
1929	Jewish Agency for Palestine established; inter-communal violence prompts British reassessment of Palestine policy
1930	Shaw Commission and Hope-Simpson report give credence to Arab claims of displacement by Jewish settlers; Passfield White Paper suggests need to control Jewish immigration and land purchases
1931	MacDonald letter effectively nullifies Passfield White Paper; Jewish Agency assumes responsibility for Haganah defence force
1933	Nazi Party assumes power in Germany
1933–1936	Fifth Aliyah raises Palestine's Jewish population to 380,000
1935	Revisionist party, led by Vladimir Jabotinsky, leaves ZO to found New Zionist Organization
1936	General strike by Palestinian Arabs develops into full revolt against British rule

1936–1939	52 Jewish 'stockade and watchtower' settlements established
1937	Peel Commission recommends partition of Palestine into Arab and Jewish states
1938	Britain withdraws partition proposal following Zionist and Arab rejections
1939	MacDonald White Paper sets British goal of establishing Palestinian state by 1949 and severely restricts Jewish immigration; Germany occupies western and central Poland, bringing 2,000,000 more Jews under Nazi rule; 136,000 Palestinian Jews volunteer for British war effort
1941–1945	Nazi Germany systematically murders 5.8 million European Jews
1942	Biltmore Programme declares Zionist goal of establishing Palestine as 'Jewish commonwealth'
1945	President Truman asks Britain to rescind 1939 White Paper and admit 100,000 Jewish refugees to Palestine; Britain refuses
1945–1948	70,000 Jewish Holocaust survivors try to run British blockade of Palestine; 5,000 succeed
1946	Britain begins deporting blockade runners to detention camps in Cyprus; Revisionists rejoin ZO, disbanding New Zionist Organization
1947	Britain announces intention to return Palestine mandate to United Nations; UNSCOP proposes new partition scheme; UN General Assembly approves establishment of Jewish and Arab states in Palestine; fighting erupts between Palestine's Jewish and Arab communities

1947–1948   Approximately 700,000 Arabs flee areas included in the Jewish state

1948   Independent State of Israel proclaimed; armies of five Arab countries invade; Israel Defence Forces established; Israel opened to unlimited Jewish immigration

1948–1951   Nearly 700,000 Jews enter Israel, more than doubling country's Jewish population.

1949   Armistice lines drawn between Israel and Egypt, Jordan, Syria and Lebanon; Israel introduces universal military conscription

1950   Law of Return offers immigrant visa to any Jew wishing to settle in Israel; Ben Gurion–Blaustein agreement commits Israel to refrain from urging US Jews to immigrate to the Jewish homeland

1951   Twenty-Third Zionist Congress adopts 'Jerusalem Programme' as supplement to 1897 'Basel Programme'

1952   Israel enacts Nationality Law giving immediate citizenship to every Jewish immigrant; Zionist Organization-Jewish Agency for Palestine Status Law merges the two bodies and defines their relationship to Israel's government

1960   ZO constitution revised; organization renamed World Zionist Organization (WZO)

1964   Palestine Liberation Organization (PLO) established, rejects legitimacy of State of Israel

1967   Six-Day War adds Old Jerusalem, West Bank, Gaza Strip, Sinai and Golan Heights to territories under

	Israel's control; calls begin for Jews to settle in newly-acquired lands
1968	Twenty-Seventh Zionist Congress revises Jerusalem Programme to emphasize 'centrality of Israel in Jewish life'
1970	Israel amends Law of Return, incorporating a definition of Jewishness derived from Jewish religious law
1971	Twenty-Eighth Zionist Congress defines immigration to Israel as primary Zionist duty, separates WZO and Jewish Agency
1973	Egypt and Syria attack Israel; Israel repulses invasion at unexpectedly high cost, prompting widespread public questioning of Labour Party leadership
1974	Gush Emunim formed to promote Jewish settlement in territories acquired by Israel in 1967
1975	UN General Assembly equates Zionism with racism
1977	Likud Party replaces Labour at head of Israeli government; religious parties in government coalition demand greater conformity between state and Jewish law, greater support for religious institutions and education; peace negotiations between Israel and Egypt begin
1979	Israel signs peace treaty with Egypt
1981	Agudat Yisrael Party demands further revision of Law of Return to ensure that diaspora conversions to Judaism are conducted according to Israeli standards

1982	Israel returns Sinai to Egypt in accordance with 1979 treaty, razing Jewish settlements and relocating settlers to areas still under Israeli control
1987–1991	Organized violence (intifada) by Palestinian Arabs in West Bank and Gaza Strip challenges Israeli control, prompting Israeli reconsideration of approach to Palestinian conflict
1991	UN General Assembly revokes 1975 equation of Zionism with racism
1992	Labour Party returns to power
1993	Oslo Accords pledge PLO recognition of Israel, Israeli transfer of authority in West Bank and Gaza Strip to Palestinian Authority, and negotiations to end Israeli–Palestinian conflict
1994	Israel signs peace treaty with Jordan
1995	Israeli Prime Minister Yitzhak Rabin assassinated by student opposed to Oslo Accords on religious grounds
2000	Israeli–Palestinian negotiations raise worldwide Jewish fears of divided Jerusalem; second intifada begins
2004	New Jerusalem Programme defines Zionism as 'the national liberation movement of the Jewish people' and commits movement to promoting a 'Jewish, Zionist, democratic, and secure State of Israel'

CHAPTER 1

The idea of a
'Jewish state'

LET'S START WITH THE BASICS.

The word 'Zionism' comes from 'Zion', one of the Hebrew Bible's names for Jerusalem. During the 1890s 'Zionism' began to be used as a designation for certain activities aimed at encouraging Jews from different parts of the world to settle close to Jerusalem, in a region many called Palestine. In August 1897, some two hundred Jews who took interest in those activities established a body called the Zionist Organization (ZO), which defined Zionism as a movement seeking 'to create for the Jewish people a home in Palestine secured by public law'. Half a century later, on 14 May 1948, representatives of the Zionist movement publicly proclaimed 'the establishment of a Jewish state in Palestine, to be called the State of Israel'. Since then the ZO has redefined its mission three times, in 1951, 1968 and 2004. In the latest redefinition it dedicated itself to 'strengthening Israel as a Jewish, Zionist, and democratic state'.

Palestine

The name 'Palestine' is probably connected with the people called Philistines in the Hebrew Bible. They lived along the south-eastern corner of the Mediterranean Sea from the twelfth through to the seventh century BCE, in an area that the Hebrew Bible called *Peleshet* and the Greek historian Herodotus *Palaistinêi*. The Romans gave the name currency during the second century CE, when they designated an administrative division they had formerly called *Iudaea* (the English 'Judea') as *Syria Palaestina*.

For over 1,500 years after the end of Roman rule, 'Palestine' sometimes designated an administrative unit with definite boundaries, sometimes (especially under the Ottoman Empire, which controlled the eastern Mediterranean between 1517 and 1917) a less specific geographical region. Jews traditionally called the same region *Erets Yisra'el* (the Land of Israel) but used Palestine when speaking European languages. Christians often referred to it as 'the Holy Land' (a designation also used in the Qur'an).

Palestine again became a clearly-defined political unit in the early 1920s, when Great Britain assumed a mandate from the League of Nations to administer the territory. From 1920 to 1922 its borders included not only the territory of the current State of Israel (including the West Bank and Gaza Strip) but that of Jordan as well. Since Hebrew and Arabic served as official languages in British mandatory Palestine alongside English, the country was also known formally as *Erets Yisra'el* and *Falastîn*. In English translations of official Hebrew documents from the period, 'Palestine' was the accepted rendering of *Erets Yisra'el*, and Jewish citizens of the country were said to be of 'Palestinian' nationality.

Following the establishment of the State of Israel in 1948, 'Palestine' increasingly became used in connection with Arab assertions of sovereignty over part or all of the former British mandatory territory west of the Jordan River.

If you think those facts tell a simple story, think again! Actually, they raise questions whose answers are not simple at all.

First, what exactly is 'the Jewish people' for whom the ZO sought a home? In the English-speaking world most people understand 'Jewish' to designate a religious group. It's fairly clear what English speakers mean when they talk about individual 'Jewish people': people who are identified with the Jewish religion to one degree or another. But to many it must sound strange to talk about 'the Jewish people' as a whole, just as it sounds strange to talk about 'the Catholic people', 'the Lutheran people' or 'the Muslim people' as discreet social groups. Talking about 'a home for the Lutheran people' somewhere in the world probably wouldn't make sense to most residents of English-speaking countries in the way that 'a home for the Polish people' or 'the Thai people' would. So what do those words suggest when applied to 'the Jewish people'?

Similarly, it isn't obvious at all what the phrase 'a Jewish state' signifies. Substituting 'Catholic' or 'Muslim' for 'Jewish' and talking about a 'Catholic state' or a 'Muslim state' won't make the concept easier to grasp. After all, what would a 'Catholic state' look like in practice? Would every citizen of the state have to be a Catholic? Would officials of the Catholic Church make the state's laws? Would Catholics be the only ones who determined what children studied in school, who voted in elections or who held public office? Would all residents have to pay taxes to support Catholic worship, even if they weren't Catholics themselves? If instead of 'Catholic' we used the word 'Jewish' in these questions and asked them about the State of Israel, the answer to each of them would be negative. In the self-proclaimed 'Jewish state' *not* all citizens are Jews; Jewish religious leaders do *not* make the country's laws; Jews are *not* the only ones who vote, occupy public office and determine school curricula; and Jewish religious institutions are *not* the only ones supported by public funds. If so, then what exactly makes Israel a 'Jewish state'?

There is also a historical problem. Does the fact that the word 'Zionism' first came to be widely used at a relatively recent moment in historical time (the 1890s) mean that the basic idea the word came to signify – that Jews from different parts of the world ought to settle in Palestine and seek a 'home' there 'secured by public law' – is itself only a bit more than a century old? The fact that the word is derived from an ancient name in the foundational text of Judaism might well suggest that the idea is much older, rooted in traditional Jewish religious ideals. Indeed, when Zionist representatives composed the State of Israel's Declaration of Independence in 1948, they contended that their movement actually dated back thousands of years:

The Land of Israel was the birthplace of the Jewish people. Here their spiritual, religious, and national identity was formed. Here they achieved independence and created a culture of national and universal significance. Here they wrote and gave the Bible to the world. Exiled from the Land of Israel, the Jewish people remained faithful to it in all the countries of their dispersion, never ceasing to pray and hope for their return and the restoration of their national freedom. Impelled by this historic association, Jews strove throughout the centuries to go back to the land of their fathers and regain their statehood.

But if that is the case, why was it only in the 1890s that an organization was founded to make that striving a reality? And why was it only during the twentieth century that the ancient hope was fulfilled?

Without answers to these questions it won't be possible to understand what Zionism is about. Fortunately, the brief capsule history in Israel's Declaration of Independence suggests where to look for them. Let's examine it more closely.

Names and histories

What does it mean to say that 'the Land of Israel was the birthplace of the Jewish people'?

In Hebrew (the language in which the Declaration of Independence was written and the dominant language in contemporary Israel), the phrase translated as 'the Jewish people' is 'ha-Am ha-Yehudi'. 'Yehudi' is an adjective meaning 'Jewish', but it is also a noun meaning 'Jew'. It is derived from the personal name *Yehudah* (Judah), who is mentioned in the biblical book of Genesis as the fourth son of the patriarch Jacob. Already in biblical times, however, *Yehudah* was also the name of a political entity. That entity, usually called Judah or Judea in English, existed from perhaps as early as 1000 BCE until the second century CE. Located in a hilly region, it was bounded in the east by the Jordan River and in the south by the Negev desert. In the west it extended to where the hills met the Mediterranean coastal plain, and in the north to a line slightly above Jerusalem and Jericho.

Sometimes Judah was an independent kingdom; at others it was a province of a larger empire. In both cases, the country's inhabitants were usually called collectively by a name derived from the place: *Yehudi* in Hebrew, *Ioudaios* in Greek, *Iudeus* in Latin. These are the names ordinarily rendered in English as 'Jew'. In other words, the label 'Jew' was originally not a religious but a political designation. It signified a person who was thought to belong to the political entity called Judah or Judea – what we might call today a 'citizen' of Judah, who lived in the country by right and could bequeath that right to later generations.

Interestingly, though, in ancient times Jews themselves didn't use the name much when speaking about themselves. More often they called themselves *'Yisra'el'*, which is the name 'Israel' in English. Like Judah, Israel was a biblical name for both a person (Judah's father, also called Jacob) and a political entity. The Bible tells of a Kingdom of Israel that reached from Judah's northern boundary all the way to the mountains of southern Lebanon. In the tenth century BCE Israel and Judah are said to have been united under a succession of kings (Saul, David and Solomon). However, after Solomon's death (around 930 BCE) Israel broke away; in 721 BCE it was absorbed into the Assyrian Empire and disappeared from the political map. However, while it had been associated with Judah, the inhabitants of the latter country had begun to call themselves *'Bnei Yisra'el'* – 'Children of Israel' or 'Israelites' – along with their northern neighbours. The name stuck even after the Kingdom of Israel vanished.

Why did Judeans prefer the name 'Israel' to one derived from their own country? We can't know for certain. It appears likely, though, that by doing so they reinforced their connection with an ancient Israelite tradition, according to which the patriarch Israel (Jacob) had inherited from his grandfather Abraham a promise from God to 'give [his] offspring the land from the River of Egypt to the Great River, the River Euphrates' (Genesis 15:18). The territory encompassed by that promise had long been called *'Erets Yisra'el'* – the Land of Israel, or the land that Israel's descendants claimed to inhabit by divine command. By including themselves among Israel's children, the Judeans thus high-lighted their claim to live where they did by right.

That claim was generally accepted by the successive empires – Babylonian, Persian, Greek and Roman – that controlled Judea for most of the interval from the Babylonian conquest in 586 BCE until around 135 CE, when the Romans renamed the province and surrounding areas *Syria Palaestina* and denied Jews any special status in it. Thus when, as a result of the Babylonian conquest, Judeans began migrating in large numbers beyond their country's borders (forming what came to be termed a 'diaspora', from the Greek word for 'scattering'), others continued to call them Jews. That practice continued even after 135, extending to the areas throughout the Middle East, North Africa, Europe and beyond in which Jews formed communities in subsequent centuries. From then on, however, the name could no longer be used in its original sense, because a political entity called Judea, to which Jews rightfully belonged, had ceased to exist. Instead it came to be used as an ethnic designation, referring to descendants of ancient Judeans anywhere in the world.

In most places throughout the centuries, that ethnic usage closely reflected observable reality. For the bulk of their history Jews were easily identifiable as a distinct social group: they often differed from the non-Jews in whose midst they lived not only in religion but in language, dress, eating habits, neighbourhoods of residence, educational and social welfare systems, and occupation. Moreover, Jews who lived in one place often shared certain cultural attributes with Jews who lived in another part of the world altogether. Jews described this situation with the help of a biblical phrase: *Am Yisra'el* – 'the People of Israel'. Like 'Children of Israel', the phrase initially referred to the descendants of Jacob to whom God was supposed to have promised a certain territory. Later it came to signify a Jewish ethnic and cultural unit that transcended political boundaries. The expression 'the Jewish people' (*ha-Am ha-Yehudi*) is simply a more modern way of designating the same entity.

This is the history that Israel's Declaration of Independence evoked when it claimed that 'the Land of Israel was the birthplace of the Jewish people'.

Jewish messianic traditions

But what of the Declaration's next assertion: 'Exiled from the Land of Israel, the Jewish people remained faithful to it in all the countries of their dispersion, never ceasing to pray and hope for their return and the restoration of their national freedom'?

The key to unpacking this claim lies in a historical-theological puzzle. On the one hand, Jewish tradition asserted that God had promised the Land of Israel to the People of Israel in perpetuity. However, beginning in the sixth century BCE a succession of foreign conquerors had overrun the country, until the Romans eventually disavowed any unique Jewish claims upon it. Jewish religious thinkers thus faced a conundrum. Did foreign conquest mean that God had similarly disavowed the ancient promise? If so, why? If not, why hadn't God – whom Jews depicted as the all-powerful creator of heaven and earth – intervened to prevent defeat?

In order to resolve this dilemma, Jewish thinkers, beginning in Roman times, developed an explanation that generations of Jews found compelling. Several biblical passages suggested that God's promise of the land had actually been conditional: God was bound to uphold it only as long as the people obeyed the special laws and commandments dictated to Moses during the Exodus from Egypt. Hence, the notion ran, the Jews' loss pointed to God's dissatisfaction with how they had kept their end of the bargain: as punishment for their failure to obey God's law, God had taken the Jews' homeland from them, effectively sending them into exile. In such a situation, Jews could only hope that one day the divine punishment would be lifted and that God would restore their mastery over the Promised Land. Indeed, prayers for restoration became part of the Jewish liturgy: even the traditional Jewish grace after meals implores a merciful God to 'break the yoke around our neck and lead us to our country with head held high'.

No doubt the authors of Israel's Declaration of Independence had prayers like this in mind when they located Zionism's roots many centuries before the ZO was founded. But if Jews had prayed consistently since Roman times to regain mastery over the territory they believed God had promised them, why was it only towards the end of the nineteenth century that they formed the organization that helped them achieve that goal? Actually, the Declaration asserted not only that Jews prayed for restoration but actively 'strove throughout the centuries to go back . . . and regain their statehood'. Was the ZO actually a late embodiment not only of a hope but of a tangible movement that had begun long before?

It turns out that when it spoke about continuous hands-on efforts by Jews to resettle and reclaim Palestine, the Declaration of Independence glossed over parts of the historical record – as political documents often do. It is true that throughout Jewish history some individual Jews left relatively more comfortable lives outside Palestine in order to satisfy a deep longing to settle in what they saw as their true homeland. However, the number of such Jews appears to have been quite small. In fact, for more than a thousand years after Muslim armies first took control of the country in 632 CE, Palestine's Jewish population declined sharply, from around 200,000 in the mid-seventh century to no more than 3,000 in 1700. Moreover, certain Jewish religious ideas actually appear to have *discouraged* Jews from trying to reclaim sovereignty there. Since restoration was possible only after God lifted the punishment of exile, Jews traditionally watched for signs that God was about to relent. They anticipated that, when the time came, God would choose a champion who would gather the Jewish people from all the lands of their dispersion, organize them to take control of the Promised Land, and lead them there in triumph. They called that anticipated champion *mashi'ah* – literally, 'the anointed one', or, as it is usually rendered in English, 'Messiah'. Once the Messiah appeared, Jews believed, the return to Palestine would be at hand. But they also believed that the timing of the Messiah's appearance was up to God alone. In fact, throughout most of their history the majority of Jewish religious leaders insisted that, except for praying and observing God's commandments, Jews neither could nor should do anything to persuade God to send the Messiah quickly. Some even warned that if Jews tried to resettle Palestine en masse before the Messiah came, God was liable to interpret their efforts as an act of rebellion and extend the punishment, making the exile last longer.

A minority understood the concepts of exile and Messiah differently, however. According to that understanding, God would send the Messiah only after Jews showed that they were prepared not merely to pray for a return to Palestine but actually to live there. Broad developments in Jewish history helped this minority view gain influence from the sixteenth century onwards; by the beginning of the eighteenth century some Jewish leaders even organized groups to settle the country. To be sure, their efforts attracted only a small following among Jews throughout the world, but they nevertheless appear to have reversed the millennium-long decline in Palestine's Jewish population. From its low point in 1700, the number of Jews in Palestine doubled over the next hundred years. The pace of growth increased even more during the nineteenth century, doubling again by 1840 and yet again by 1880, when the country's Jewish population reached some 24,000. Still, that number represented barely half a per cent of the estimated 4.75 million Jews throughout the world at the time. And although the Jews' proportion of the overall population of Palestine was increasing, it still barely exceeded 5 per cent of the country's 450,000 residents.

The minority messianic tradition that inspired the increased immigration of the eighteenth and nineteenth centuries revealed certain characteristics that also figured in the Zionist movement. In particular, both depended upon an ethos of activism – one that encouraged Jews to settle and take control of Palestine through their own efforts, without waiting for divine intervention. But there were also fundamental differences between Zionism and activist messianism – differences that call the connection between the two projects into question.

The most important differences were the divergent goals Zionists and active messianists attached to their respective programmes. Jews seeking to hasten the coming of the Messiah expected that divinely-endorsed re-establishment of Jewish sovereignty in Palestine would catalyse a much more extensive process, one that would usher in a totally new era for the entire universe, in which all laws of physical and biological existence would be replaced by a cosmic reality altogether different from any previously known. They hoped that they would soon be able to abandon the tribulations of what they called 'this world' for the anticipated bliss of 'the world to come'. The first Zionists, in contrast, harboured no such hope. They did not think about a new cosmic era. Instead they saw the creation of 'a home in Palestine for the Jewish people secured by public law' as a way to bring Jews immediate benefits in the world they already knew. Put another way, Zionists were initially far less concerned with Jews' traditional religious aspirations than they were with what they considered their current material needs.

In addition, Zionists thought that those material needs could best be met by actions aimed at changing not so much God's attitude towards Jews as the way other human beings related to them. Messianic ideas didn't seem to tell them how to accomplish this goal, so they didn't figure in most Zionists' writings. In fact, Jewish religious authorities (rabbis) were at first not terribly prominent in the Zionist movement. On the contrary, when it was established only a handful of rabbis expressed support for the ZO, whose most prominent figures claimed authority to represent 'the Jewish people' by virtue of their familiarity with contemporary European politics and culture instead of with the fundamental texts of Judaism. Indeed, most rabbis actively opposed Zionist efforts.

These facts suggest that, prayers for restoration notwithstanding, Zionism might be better understood as a departure from traditional Jewish ways of looking at the world than as an extension of ancient Jewish religious values. And if Zionism really does embody more a modern than an ancient idea, then it makes sense to look for its origins around the time the word gained currency, not centuries before.

The European seedbed: states, citizens and nations

What happened to Jews in the nineteenth century that could have prompted the new direction that the founding of the ZO signified?

It turns out that the century following the French Revolution of 1789 was an especially stressful and turbulent time in Jewish history. The strains that Jews experienced resulted largely from powerful changes that took place throughout all of Europe during the same interval – changes that radically altered ideas about how states, societies and individuals, Jews and non-Jews alike, ought to relate to one another.

Before the French Revolution, most Europeans believed states to be the creations of the ruling families that governed them. Rulers were supposed to rule their territories more or less as they saw fit, with only limited regard for the wishes of their subjects. Some subjects, however – nobles, clergymen, townspeople and artisans, but usually not the peasants who made up the majority of the population – were entitled to have their wishes represented by legally-constituted corporations or estates, which negotiated with rulers on behalf of all their members collectively. On the basis of those negotiations rulers would grant each corporation a charter of rights that determined the duties and privileges of the subjects who belonged to it. Under this system there was no expectation that rulers would treat the different estates equally. On the contrary, in the corporation-based state, social inequality was considered normal and proper.

The French Revolution ushered in a novel political model. According to the new ideal, states were to be constituted not by dynastic rulers but by the entire body of individuals who were subject to the state's jurisdiction. Those individuals were usually referred to collectively as 'the people'; those who belonged to 'the people' of a particular state were often said to be 'citizens' of that country. The French Revolutionary model also provided that citizens should stand in more or less equal relationship to the state authorities. It thus left no room for corporations whose charters determined the political status of their members. Instead, citizens and state authorities were to relate directly to one another, without mediation by corporate bodies.

During the nineteenth century, citizen-based states replaced corporation-based states as the norm in most of Europe. European society thus had to adjust to the new model. Not surprisingly, different sectors of society – nobles and clergy, merchants and artisans, peasants and labourers – adjusted differently, depending upon what they gained or lost as a result of the change. In fact, throughout Europe the nineteenth century was a time when clashes among different social groups trying to gain the greatest possible advantages for themselves during the transition to citizen-based states were common.

For Jews, adjusting to the new system was not a simple matter. On the whole they had done rather well under the pre-revolutionary arrangement. Wherever they lived, rulers had recognized them as constituting a corporation of their own, entitled to its own charter of rights. The charters that gave Jews the right to reside in a particular territory usually regulated many features of their daily lives, including where they could set up their homes, what they could do for a living, sometimes even what they could wear or whom they could employ. Also, Jews usually had to pay rulers for the rights the charters granted them. But on the other hand, the charters also gave Jews broad autonomy in managing their internal communal affairs. More importantly, they obligated rulers to protect Jews – to make certain that they were physically secure. Generally speaking, rulers were willing to strike such a bargain whenever they sensed that the Jews who settled on their lands would bring them economic advantage.

Most of the time both sides lived up to their end of the contract. Jews paid their taxes regularly, made few demands on the state treasury and performed economic services that rulers found valuable, while rulers kept them safe. True, there were several well-known instances during the Middle Ages when one ruler or another came to see the presence of Jews as a liability instead of a benefit. In those cases Jews found themselves facing expulsion, confiscation of property and sometimes even physical violence. But on the whole, the system of contractual arrangements between Jews and territorial rulers provided Jews with a stable and secure existence.

Would Jews do as well in citizen-based states? The answer was not obvious. The new ideal, with its insistence on equality before the law, made it impossible for them to continue living in their countries of residence on the basis of a special contract with the state authorities: either they became citizens like everyone else, or they could claim no legal right to reside in the state's territory. However, whether or not they became citizens was not up to Jews alone: in virtually every European state that moved from the corporate to the citizen-based model in the decades following the French Revolution, the citizens as a whole had to decide whether Jews ought to be admitted into their ranks. For Jews, that situation was disquieting. Under the pre-revolutionary arrangement, their physical security in any given location had depended mainly (although not entirely, and not always) on the relations they maintained with one person – the ruler. Indeed, their right to reside in a particular place was usually determined by what one single individual thought about them. In citizen-based states, in contrast, the Jews' right of residence and physical security (not to mention their material well-being and social standing) depended on what the general body of citizens thought about them. In other words, Jews now had to submit themselves to the judgement of their non-Jewish neighbours and to win their approval if they wished to enjoy the benefits of citizenship.

Jews could not take approval for granted. Although pre-revolutionary rulers may have been willing to tolerate them because of their economic usefulness, many other segments of the European population had historically seen them as unwelcome competitors or exploiters. Those negative perceptions had long been reinforced by the general suspicion that attached to their refusal to accept the Christian religion. As a result, many Europeans harboured doubts about whether Jews were worthy of being counted among the constitutors of the states where they lived. In fact, all over Europe, throughout the nineteenth century, the alleged merits and demerits of Jews, the Jewish religion and Jewish culture became subjects of more intense public scrutiny and debate than ever before, in order to determine whether they deserved to be counted as citizens or not.

The course and outcome of those debates varied from country to country. However, by the final third of the nineteenth century two broad patterns emerged. In most of the countries of Western and Central Europe – including Germany (where some 600,000 Jews lived in 1900), Great Britain (250,000), the Netherlands (104,000) and France (100,000) – Jews eventually did enter the citizenry as equals (although vocal and sometimes powerful groups opposed this arrangement and worked to undo it). Most of the Jews in these countries responded to their inclusion by gradually abandoning the distinct cultural characteristics that had set them apart from their neighbours in earlier times. They began to think of themselves as Germans, Britons or Frenchmen like any others, distinguishable as Jews solely by virtue of their religion. This was the context in which the word 'Jewish' first acquired the exclusively religious connotation that contemporary English speakers usually attach to it.

Demography of the Jews

The number of Jews in the world and their geographical distribution has fluctuated widely throughout history. In the first century CE there may have been as many as eight million Jews, most of whom lived in Palestine, Babylonia and the eastern Mediterranean region. That number declined steadily, until by the fifteenth century the world's Jewish population probably dipped below one million before beginning an upward swing.

In the Middle Ages most Jews continued to live in the eastern Mediterranean, with 70 per cent inhabiting regions with a Muslim majority. Although Jews settled permanently in Europe north of the Alps in the tenth century, those areas did not become the Jewish demographic centre until early modern times. European economic expansion helped concentrate more than four million of the world's 4.75 million Jews in the continent by 1850. However, expulsions from parts of Western Europe from the sixteenth through to the eighteenth century made the continent's eastern regions the dominant site of Jewish settlement. A general population explosion in those regions during the second half of the nineteenth century saw Jewish numbers increase as well, rising to well over seven million by 1900 (out of 11.5 million in the world), despite intensive emigration to the Americas after 1880. In some parts of Eastern Europe Jews made up 12–14 per cent of the total population; some cities even had Jewish majorities. Elsewhere Jews seldom surpassed 1 per cent of the total.

By 1939 world Jewry exceeded 16 million – its highest total ever. The Nazi Holocaust reduced the number by a third and ended Europe's demographic dominance. In 2000 there were some 13 million Jews in the world, including six million in the United States and five million in Israel.

At the time, however, fewer than 15 per cent of Europe's nearly nine million Jews lived in states of this type. The overwhelming majority lived instead in the two great multinational empires of Eastern Europe – Austria-Hungary (with more than two million Jews) and Russia (with over five million). In those countries the situation was far more complicated, mainly because neither of them survived the transition from corporate to citizen-based states intact. The reason why neither Russia nor Austria-Hungary transformed themselves according to the model that took root in Western and Central Europe was that no unified 'people', consisting of all the empire's residents, emerged in either of them to wrest power from their rulers and reconstitute them on the basis of a common citizenship. Instead, the initiative in transforming those empires into something other than dynastic, corporate-based states fell to various subsets of their populations that split mainly along ethnolinguistic lines, including Poles, Czechs, Hungarians, Lithuanians, Slovaks, Croats and Ukrainians. Instead of trying to reorganize the two empires as single, unified citizen-based states (in which all former subjects of the Austrian emperor or Russian tsar ruled together on a equal basis), spokesmen for these groups advocated dividing them into a series of smaller states, in each of which one ethnolinguistic group would comprise the bulk of the citizenry that constituted it. In the end they prevailed: after the First World War the empires were broken apart, and seven new states – Estonia, Latvia, Lithuania, Poland, Czechoslovakia, Hungary and Yugoslavia – were carved out of their territories.

The argument usually advanced in favour of dividing the empires in this way was based on a variant of the citizenship idea, one that not every citizen-based state affirmed. The variant asserted first of all that what ultimately gave the people of any country the right to govern it was not simply the fact that they lived together in a single political unit but the fact that they shared a common language and history. That common language and history were thought to define homogeneous 'peoples' or 'nations'. In other words, not citizenries ('the people') were regarded as the legitimate rulers of states, but specific 'peoples' whose identities were supposed to have been formed long before the states they were entitled to rule had been created. In fact, exponents of this notion maintained that every 'people' or 'nation' has an inalienable right to constitute a state 'of its own' – one whose primary purpose is to serve the collective needs and interests of the nation that established it. Five of the new states created after the First World War – Hungary, Poland and the three Baltic countries – conceived of themselves in this fashion, even though all of them had many residents who did not belong to the dominant national group.

Although this idea about how states ought to be constituted was put into practice only after the First World War (when it was explicitly endorsed by the Paris Peace Conference in accordance with US President Woodrow Wilson's principle of 'self-determination'), it had figured prominently in public debate throughout Eastern Europe during the final third of the nineteenth century. In fact, during that time it became clear to growing numbers of observers that Russia and Austria-Hungary were bound to be reconstituted sooner or later and that movements representing those empires' 'nations' would play a key role in reshaping them. The region's millions of Jews were well attuned to this prospect, and from the 1880s some of them began to think about how Jews might best preserve their physical security and material welfare when the expected realignment came.

The Zionist movement was born of such thinking.

The logic of Jewish nationalism

For many Jews, especially in Eastern Europe, the prospect of 'national' states posed challenges no less formidable than those presented by the citizen-based model. Unlike their co-religionists to the west, most East European Jews continued to be set apart from non-Jews by a range of social and cultural characteristics. They spoke a different language – Yiddish – based upon an early medieval German dialect with extensive admixtures from Hebrew, Aramaic, the Slavic languages, Latin and old French. They earned their livelihoods mainly in commerce and artisanry, in contrast to the surrounding heavily agricultural non-Jewish populations. Their habits of dress, grooming and eating made most of them immediately identifiable. They maintained their own networks of schools and charitable institutions. And they arranged their lives according to a different calendar from that of their neighbours. As a result, the newly-crystallizing nations of Eastern Europe tended to think that Jews did not belong to them: 'Polish Jews', for example, might live in a territory called 'Poland', but they were not 'Poles' – certainly not in the sense that Jews who lived in France might claim to be Frenchmen. Similarly, the national movements of many of the East European peoples excluded Jews – sometimes tacitly, sometimes explicitly – from the ranks of those whose needs their hoped-for states were meant to serve. And because at the time there was no large contiguous territory in Eastern Europe (or anywhere else in the world) where Jews formed a majority of the population, dividing Austria-Hungary and Russia into 'national' states meant that Jews would live everywhere under governments whose obligations towards them came after the ones they owed their constituting nations.

In such a situation, what were Jews to do? Some Jewish leaders advocated mass migration to the citizen-based states of Western Europe and the Americas, where Jews might enjoy better prospects for integration and acceptance. Others thought it best to work together with non-Jewish liberals to transform Russia and Austria-Hungary into citizen-based states along West European lines, where only 'the people' as a whole, and not particular 'peoples', would be politically significant. Still others saw little possibility of accomplishing this goal until certain fundamental transformations in the societies of those empires took place. Those Jews were strongly attracted to socialism, because the fundamental socialist principle that the proper relationship be-tween states and societies ought to be determined by class instead of ethnolinguistic identity seemed to offer them a greater chance of inclusion among those whom states were supposed to serve.

On the other hand, growing numbers of Jews suspected that nation-based states would soon become the norm worldwide, perhaps even replacing existing citizen-based states. They figured that in a world of nation-based states, the best way for Jews to maximize their well-being was to claim that they com-prised a nation themselves and that therefore they too had an inalienable right to constitute a state that would define serving their collective needs and interests as one of its fundamental purposes. This idea came to be known as *Jewish nationalism*.

In the reality of Eastern Europe at the time, the claim that Jews should be counted as a nation (comparable to Poles, Lithuanians, Czechs or Slovaks) instead of as a religious group (comparable to Catholic or Orthodox Christians) made sense, at least to a point. The principal criteria of 'nationhood', as the term was understood at the time, were language and history. Most East European Jews habitually spoke and wrote a language of their own, and they could point to collective origins and history different from those of their non-Jewish neighbours. Moreover, if other national movements excluded Jews from their ranks, then logically Jews *had* to comprise a nation of their own. On the other hand, though, non-Jewish East European ethnolin-guistic groups who claimed the right to establish states 'of their own' could point to some part of the world where most of their members lived and where they formed a majority of the popula-tion. Jews could not point to such a territory. That fact weakened their claim to national status in the eyes of many non-Jews.

Some Jewish nationalists maintained that being a majority in some territory was at most only a secondary qualification for nationhood; thus Jews could still be considered a nation, even if there wasn't any one territory with which they were primarily associated. They also argued that states did not necessarily have to 'belong' to one nation alone: two or more nations could legitimately join together to establish a single, multinational state, which would support the needs and interests of all the nations that constituted it. In other words, they claimed, if a national state were created in areas where Poles formed the majority but Jews lived in large numbers, both the Polish and Jewish nations should be considered constitutors of that state, and both should be entitled to claim its backing. The aim of Jewish nationalism, in their view, should be to work towards the reorganization of Austria-Hungary and Russia on such a multinational basis.

Other Jewish nationalists, in contrast, held that Jews would do better to find some territory beyond Europe, open to immigration, where they could relocate en masse and eventually become a majority. Once they did so, these nationalists explained, Jews would be able legitimately to constitute their own mononational state. That state would be a 'Jewish state' in the same sense that a reconstituted Poland would be a 'Polish state' – its primary purpose would be to advance the collective interests of 'the Jewish people' (or 'the Jewish nation'), just as a 'Polish state' would advance the collective interests of 'the Polish people'.

This was the basic idea of Zionism. Its fundamental impulse was less an ancient Jewish religious imperative than fear that the large majority of the world's Jews would soon find themselves without adequate protection for their lives and livelihoods. That fear had a real basis in the spread of national movements in nineteenth-century Eastern Europe. By adopting the premisses of those movements instead of fighting them, Zionists hoped to make the nationalist current work to Jews' advantage instead of their detriment. In other words, had the concept of national states not taken root in Europe towards the end of the nineteenth century, it is doubtful that a body like the ZO would have come into being at that time. Similarly, the language of Israel's Declaration of Independence – which asserted that 'it is the natural right of the Jewish people to lead, as do all other nations, an independent existence in its sovereign State' – must be understood first of all in light of basic nineteenth-century European concepts of states, nations and citizenship.

Those concepts cannot explain everything in the Declaration, however. For one thing, the idea that, in a world of national states, it was incumbent upon Jews to resettle in a territory where they could form a majority and create a national state of their own does not tell us why that territory had to be Palestine. Indeed, some early Zionists thought about other territories as well. Were traditional Jewish religious imperatives central in directing Zionist attentions to Palestine specifically, or did more immediate historical developments play a decisive role in this feature of the movement as well?

The capsule history in the Declaration of Independence doesn't shed light on that question. To answer it we need to examine the writings and deeds of the early Zionists themselves.

Recommended reading

A collection of basic documents concerning the history of Zionism, the State of Israel and the Arab–Israeli conflict is *The*

Israel–Arab Reader, edited by Walter Laqueur and Barry Rubin (sixth revised edition, London: Penguin, 2001). The quotations from the 1897 self-definition of the ZO and Israel's Declaration of Independence can be found there. The three post-1948 incarnations of the ZO's programme (from 1951, 1968 and 2004) can be obtained via the website of the American Zionist Movement: http://www.azm.org/jprog.shtml.

Scholarly opinion concerning significant aspects of the history of ancient Israel and Judea is in flux, and because many find contemporary political implications in the way the ancient history is narrated, disagreements are often intense. A suitably restrained, current and accessible introduction to the subject and some of its difficulties is the essay by Adele Berlin and Marc Zvi Brettler, 'Historical and Geographical Background to the Bible', in *The Jewish Study Bible* (Oxford: Oxford University Press, 2004), pp. 2048–62.

The classic scholarly exposition of Jewish ideas about the Messiah is the essay by Gershom Scholem, 'Toward an Understanding of the Messianic Idea in Judaism', in his collection, *The Messianic Idea in Judaism and Other Essays on Jewish Spirituality* (New York: Schocken Books, 1971), pp. 1–36. Some of Scholem's central ideas have been revised in Moshe Idel, *Messianic Mystics* (New Haven: Yale University Press, 1998). The points of contact between messianism and Zionism are analysed incisively in Aviezer Ravitzky, *Messianism, Zionism, and Jewish Religious Radicalism* (Chicago: University of Chicago Press, 1996).

The development of modern states and their relation to 'nations' is the subject of a vast literature. A useful starting point is Hagen Schulze, *States, Nations, and Nationalism from the Middle Ages to the Present* (Oxford: Blackwell, 1996). The East European aspects of that development are treated in Ivan T. Berend, *Decades of Crisis: Central and Eastern Europe Before World War II* (Berkeley: University of California Press, 1998). A lucid, concise introduction to how Jews responded to the transformations of the nineteenth century is Ezra Mendelsohn, *On Modern Jewish Politics* (New York: Oxford University Press, 1993).

Historians identified with Zionism have developed their own characteristic narrative of their movement's history and its connection to other aspects of the Jewish past. A classic example is Ben Zion Dinur, *Israel and the Diaspora* (Philadelphia: Jewish Publication Society, 1969).

CHAPTER 2

Crystallization of a movement, 1881–1897

ONE OF THE KEY WRITINGS ZIONISTS CITE when they recall the history of their movement was penned in 1881 by Perez Smolenskin. A leading Jewish intellectual of his day, Smolenskin had been among the first to call Jews a 'nation' in the contemporary European sense. The essay that most endeared him to Zionists, however – a short piece entitled 'Let Us Search Our Ways' (in Hertzberg, 1997: 148–53) – did not touch on political questions. Instead, it offered a new perspective on Palestine's significance in Jewish life. Smolenskin's article thus provides insight into how Zionist attentions came to focus on Palestine instead of other territories.

Perez Smolenskin (1840?–1885)

Born in a village near the Russian city of Mogilev (today Mahilëŭ in Belarus), Smolenskin became, at age 13, the youngest student in the renowned *yeshiva* (academy for advanced Jewish religious studies) of Shklov (Škloŭ). Against school policies, but like a growing number of *yeshiva* students in his day, he read not only sacred Jewish texts but writings by a small group of modernizers who urged Jews to master European languages. Commitment to the modernizers' agenda led to an eventual break with traditional Jewish ways of life; between 1858 and 1868 Smolenskin lived in Vitebsk (Vicebsk), Yekaterinoslav (Dnipropetrovs'k, Ukraine) and Odessa, working at various jobs while acquiring, on his own, a secular European education. After beginning in Odessa to write for a Hebrew-language newspaper, he decided to launch a Hebrew journal of his own. Difficulties securing a permit for his enterprise prompted him to leave the Russian Empire. In 1868, from his new residence in Vienna, he launched the monthly *Hashahar* (The Dawn).

Hashahar was the premier Hebrew intellectual review of its day, publishing articles on the latest developments in European philosophy and science, commentary on Jewish and European public affairs, and *belles-lettres*. Smolenskin was also known for his satirical novels and short stories, many of which parodied the parochial ways of small-town East European Jewry, and his home in Vienna was a gathering place for devotees of modern Hebrew literature and for young people aspiring to careers in Hebrew journalism.

Palestine and Jewish migration

Smolenskin wrote at an anxiety-ridden crossroads in Jewish history. Over the previous two decades East European Jews, along with many segments of the societies in which they lived, had seen their traditional sources of livelihood undermined by industrialization. A population explosion had exacerbated distress, so that by the late 1870s many Jews and non-Jews, no longer able to make ends meet, were migrating abroad. Among

Jews the pace of migration quickened in the spring of 1881 following a wave of mob assaults, commonly called pogroms, in the south-western provinces of the Russian Empire. The pogroms were catalysed by the assassination of Tsar Alexander II in March 1881, when rioters blamed Jews for killing their sovereign, using the murder as an excuse to give violent expression to recently exacerbated resentments. Local police, usually poorly-trained and equipped, were often ineffective and at times dilatory in protecting the victims. Public opinion, too, responded in a way many Jews interpreted as hostile, and false rumours spread among them that the new tsar himself had approved and perhaps even ordered the attacks. Within weeks thousands of Jewish refugees from the affected areas began fleeing across the Austrian border, and Jewish leaders pondered whether to encourage a mass exodus. Indeed, although the pogroms of 1881–1882 took their principal toll in property, not in lives, fear for the future permeated Russian Jewry as never before.

Smolenskin favoured mass emigration. To his mind, hostile portrayals of Jews in Russian newspapers over the previous two decades had irreversibly set non-Jews against their Jewish neighbours, to the point where Jews would never be left in peace in the Russian Empire. Therefore, he concluded, monies should be raised and organizations created to help the major portion of Russian Jews leave the country. He was hardly the only Jewish spokesman to adopt such a position. However, Smolenskin added two novel ideas to the discussion. First, he suggested, emigrants ought to resettle collectively, not individually; as he put it, 'it would be best for people who are leaving one country to migrate together to the same new land, for they could then understand and help one another'. His second idea was even bolder: 'If the wave of emigration is to direct itself to one place, surely no other country in the world is conceivable except Palestine.'

Smolenskin may have been the first person to propose organized mass Jewish settlement in Palestine not as a messianic vision but as the preferred solution to an immediate material problem. In his essay he noted that recent investigations by unnamed non-Jewish 'experts' suggested that the country could support 'all those [Jews] who might wish to take refuge there' – at least a million, probably many more. He foresaw ample opportunity for Jews to earn livelihoods as farmers, merchants and manufacturers; in particular, he believed, 'settlers could prosper by establishing factories for glass and allied products, for the sand of the country is of high quality'. Indeed, to his mind Palestine's prospects for economic development, coupled with its relative proximity and associations with the Jewish past, made it preferable to North and South America as destinations for Jewish migrants *on purely practical grounds*. Therefore, he concluded, Jews throughout the world with the necessary financial resources and organizational abilities should join forces 'to buy land [in Palestine] and let Jews settle on it to begin a new life'.

Notice: Smolenskin did not offer a vision of a 'Jewish state' in Palestine or even of 'national rebirth' for Jews there; he sought only 'to provide bread in a land in which there is hope that those who labour on it will find rest'. In retrospect it may seem curious that economic rather than sentimental considerations led him to favour what many westerners perceived as an impoverished backwater of the decaying Ottoman Empire over American opportunity. At the time, though, there were good reasons for Jews to view Palestine not only as the Promised Land but as a land of genuine promise as well. Since the 1850s the country had experienced an economic upturn, thanks largely to the establishment of steamship links between Palestine and major Mediterranean ports, which helped draw the region into the broader European economy. Western businessmen seeking investment opportunities were visiting in growing numbers, as were Christian tourists to the Holy Land (like those immortalized in Mark Twain's 1869 travelogue, *The Innocents Abroad*). This fresh interest was reflected in the establishment of new institutions by (and often for) westerners, especially on the outskirts of Jerusalem. In 1860 the Russian Orthodox Church built a cathedral, hospital and hostel for pilgrims on a former Ottoman parade ground just west of the city walls. Over the next decade German missionaries erected a hospital, an orphanage and a school for local girls farther outside the city, while German colonists established settlements near Jerusalem, Jaffa and Haifa. French missionaries soon followed suit, erecting a large monastery in 1874 and a convent in 1880. In 1881 American and Swedish Christians formed an American Colony north of Jerusalem's Damascus Gate.

These developments were widely reported in newspapers that Smolenskin and other East European Jewish intellectuals read. So, too, was information about Ottoman efforts to bolster Palestine's infrastructure and encourage further development. Jaffa and Jerusalem were joined by a telegraph line in 1865 and a wagon road two years later; by 1880 plans to build a railroad were underway. Perhaps even more significantly, East European Jews knew that Jews from Jerusalem had recently established neighbourhoods of their own outside the city walls, some of which strove to become economically self-sustaining through agriculture and industry. They also knew that wealthy West European Jews had recently taken a philanthropic interest in projects aimed at leading their co-religionists in Palestine to economic self-sufficiency. Hearing about such seemingly intense activity evidently persuaded Smolenskin that funds would be available to support his idea.

Smolenskin's suggestion might have sounded persuasive for other reasons too. In his day the idea was common that living standards of the urban poor could be improved through organized agricultural settlement. From that perspective, East European Jews experiencing the displacements of early indus-trialization seemed likely candidates for programmes aimed at moving them onto the land. Moreover, in the prevailing European hierarchy of values, farming and artisanry were more highly regarded than the petty commerce in which East Euro-pean Jews were concentrated: the former were termed 'produc-tive' occupations, while merchants were often castigated as 'exploiters' who 'lived off the labour of others'. 'Productivizing' Jews thus appeared to many as a way to improve not only their material well-being but their image as well, mitigating tensions between them and their neighbours.

Both Jews and non-Jews displayed periodic enthusiasm for 'productivization' schemes predicated on moving Jews to rural settlements of their own. Until 1866 the Russian government actually allocated a portion of tax revenues paid by Jews to devel-oping such settlements; in that year about 40,000 Jews lived in farming communes designated especially for them, mostly in the Ukrainian parts of the Empire. Subsequently the French Jewish organization Alliance Israélite Universelle purchased farmland in Russia and trained Jews to work it. When the question of emigration took centre stage on the Jewish communal agenda after 1881, the Alliance and other western Jewish agencies connected agricultural settlement with relocation overseas; between 1881 and 1900 some 50 colonies and training schools for Jewish farmers were established in rural areas of North and South America, including Louisiana, Oregon and the Argentine pampas. The initial settlers in those colonies migrated there in groups, following the model set by non-Jewish agricultural colonists from Europe (like the Amish, the Amana Inspirationists and similar communities with a common ethnoreligious identity) who had come to the New World in previous decades.

In other words, Smolenskin was hardly a pie-eyed idealist dreaming an improbable dream. He proposed a solution to difficulties facing East European Jewry in terms that were well known and accepted among educated Europeans of his day. He had every reason to expect that advocacy of Palestine as a target for organized Jewish migration would be given serious attention.

From theory to practice

Was it?

According to best estimates, some 25,000 Jews left Europe for Palestine between 1881 and 1899, the majority from the Russian Empire in the immediate aftermath of the pogroms. That is not a trivial figure, considering that between 1881 and 1884 about the same number of Jews left Russia for the United States (although over the entire 1881–1899 interval Palestine was the destination of fewer than 3 per cent of Jews who moved from Europe to another continent). It appears, though, that only a small minority of Jewish immigrants to Palestine behaved in a way that would suggest they had taken Smolenskin's message to heart. About four-fifths seem to have migrated for much the same reasons as the 12,000 or so Jews who had settled there between 1840 and 1880 – religious conviction. The remaining fifth was divided almost equally between those who took up commercial or professional occupations and those who worked the land. Between 1881 and 1890 the latter founded 13 new agricultural settlements, with about 350 families engaged in actual farming.

Most of the agricultural settlers arrived in Palestine in organized groups that had spent months or years arranging the move – recruiting members, raising funds, purchasing land for homes and farms, drawing plans for buildings, assigning plots and arranging transportation. Dozens of such groups formed throughout Russia and Romania during the early 1880s, almost always through the initiative of a handful of Jews in a particular town who, like Smolenskin, looked to Palestine primarily for its economic prospects. Soon the groups became known by a generic Hebrew name – *Hibbat Tsiyon* (fondness for Zion) societies; their members called themselves *Hovevei Tsiyon* (enthusiasts for Zion). They hardly constituted a movement in any meaningful sense: there was still no organizational connection between them, and although reliable membership figures are lacking, it is certain that their adherents were few and scattered. Nevertheless, the fact that they mobilized even limited support suggests that Smolenskin's was not a solitary voice crying in the wilderness.

But Smolenskin was not the only one whose ideas were influencing the nascent Hibbat Tsiyon groups. Where Smolenskin had concerned himself with immediate practical questions connected with migration, other Jewish intellectuals analysed why so many Jews were feeling impelled to move in the first place.

One analysis that made an especially powerful impression was offered by Moshe Leib Lilienblum (1843–1910), whose no-holds-barred, self-revelatory autobiography, *Youthful Sins*, published in 1876 when he was 33, had already made him a culture hero among growing numbers of young East European Jews. Unlike Smolenskin, who attributed current violence to recent agitation, Lilienblum saw the roots of the pogroms in what he took to be a constant fact of Jewish history:

Since we went into exile, from the time our homeland was destroyed [by Rome], and even in [ancient] Alexandria, while we still had our independence, we have been foreigners . . . abandoned foundlings, uninvited guests. During the age of faith we were foreigners in Europe because of our religion; now, in the age of nationalism, we are foreign because of our ethnic origins. We are Semites among Aryans, children of Shem among children of Japhet, a Palestinian tribe in lands belonging to the peoples of Europe. . . . Who would let a stranger into his house as if he were part of the family? (Lilienblum, 1970: 2/196)

This assessment, rooted in the ideas about 'nations' then coming into fashion in Eastern Europe and about prospects for Jews in an environment where national movements played an increasingly central role in politics, prompted Lilienblum to think of Palestine as the proper destination for Jewish emigrants, but for different reasons and with different aims than Smolenskin had suggested:

Why should we go to America, where we will still be foreigners, and not to our ancestral homeland? . . . [Palestine] can be our salvation forever! . . . Our aim must be to stop being foreigners, and once we return bit by bit to the land of our forebears we shall no longer be so.

That is what is most important! . . . It is amazing that even those who have advised going to our ancestral homeland have not yet considered the issue from the perspective of this overall situation of ours – one that requires us to stop being strangers, something we can accomplish only in the land of our forebears. (197)

Thus Lilienblum urged Jews to 'purchase plots and estates in great quantity and gradually to create permanent settlements . . . the way that all other nations live in their ancestral homelands'. The thought that he had discovered 'the straight and certain road to saving our people and its status as a nation forever' (199) made him set aside his career and devote the remaining three decades of his life to making his vision a reality.

Lilienblum's initial vision did not include a 'Jewish state', however, any more than did Smolenskin's. On the contrary, he explained, 'control of the government is not the most important thing, but citizenship rooted in history' (197) – that is, acknowledgment that Jews were not strangers in Palestine but resided there by right. But at least one of his readers took issue with him on that point. Leo Pinsker accepted Lilienblum's premise that recent attacks upon Jews were but the latest manifestation of an age-old phenomenon: 'the Jewish people has no fatherland of its own . . . it is everywhere a guest, and nowhere at home' (in Hertzberg, 1997: 183). But for him a 'fatherland' necessarily included 'a government and accredited representatives'. In fact, he thought, it was precisely the lack of such political institutions that engendered not only disrespect for Jews among other peoples but fear of them as well. In a pamphlet entitled *Autoemancipation*, published in September 1882, he explained why.

Leo Pinsker (1821–1891)

Pinsker was born in the Polish town of Tomaszów Lubelski (then part of the Russian Empire), but he grew up in Odessa. Unusually for Russian Jews of his generation (and unlike Smolenskin and Lilienblum, who were a generation younger), he was given a secular education, graduating from Odessa University with a degree in law and Moscow University with a degree in medicine (one of the first Jews to do either). He became a prominent physician in Odessa and took an active role in Jewish public affairs, helping to found the first Russian-language Jewish newspapers, *Razsvet* (Daybreak) and *Sion*, in the early 1860s. He was also active in the Society for the Spread of Education among the Jews of Russia, which promoted integration of Jews into Russian society.

The pogroms of 1881 moved him to question the possibility of integration and advocate organized mass Jewish emigration from Russia, preferably to a single country. During an 1882 trip to Western Europe to raise funds for emigrants he formulated the ideas published in *Autoemancipation* later that year. For the remaining nine years of his life he was the towering figure among the early Hovevei Tsiyon.

Jews were feared, Pinsker believed, because they were a historical anomaly. In his view, although they had once constituted a political entity of their own according to a model common among ancient peoples, they had broken with that model once their independence was lost: instead of disappearing as a recognizable group (in the way that, say, Carthaginians were no longer identified as such within several generations of the Roman destruction of Carthage in 146 BCE), Jews 'continued to exist as a nation in the spiritual sense' – that is, they were perceived as a 'nation' even though they lacked 'most attributes that serve to identify' such a group, including 'a common language, customs, and collective connection to a particular space' (Pinsker, 1936: 6, 8). That anomalous situation, he claimed, made the Jewish 'nation' seem like a disembodied spirit, 'one of the dead walking among the living', which in turn made it the object of ineradicable dread:

This ghostlike appearance . . . of a people without unity or organization, without territory or cohesion, no longer alive but wandering among the living . . . could not but make a unique, strange impression upon the imagination of the nations. And if the fear of ghosts is something inborn . . . why wonder that it turned up . . . at the sight of this nation, dead but still alive? (8–9)

Pinsker's analysis left only two possibilities for eliminating fear of the Jewish ghost: quash the fear or restore the body. Pinsker had no hope for the former: he believed that the habit of treating Jews as 'a heterogeneous element that no nation can stomach' (5) had become so ingrained in the collective European psyche as to make it impossible to overcome. Hence his operative conclusion: 'As long as we lack a home of our own like the other nations have, we shall have to abandon the noble hope of being counted as human beings of equal worth' (21–2). For him, a 'home like the other nations have' meant a state – an internationally-recognized entity, sovereign over a defined territory, empowered to conduct diplomatic relations with all other states on behalf of the Jewish people as a whole.

In theory it didn't matter to Pinsker where that home was. In fact, he offered two different suggestions: a small territory in North America or a slice of 'Asiatic Turkey'. Yet from the beginning he seems to have found the latter more palatable, guessing that the former would prove unfeasible for economic and political reasons. In 'Palestine or Syria' he suspected that large tracts of suitable land were available for purchase and that the diplomatic moment might be right to induce the Ottoman Sultan to agree to a 'sovereign [Jewish] pashalik' there. Besides, organized groups of Jewish migrants to parts of the world other than Palestine didn't seem to take his ideas to heart, whereas among early Hovevei Tsiyon he found a ready audience. Even before his pamphlet appeared, in June 1882, sixteen young Jews affiliated with a Hibbat Tsiyon society in Kharkov known as *Bilu* (an acronym derived from the Hebrew text of Isaiah 2:5 – 'House of Jacob, Let us go'), who were passing through Istanbul on their way to Palestine, had already issued a call to their 'brothers and sisters in Exile' to join them in seeking the Sultan's agreement for 'a home in our country', or at least 'a state within a larger state, the internal administration to be ours ... and to act with the Turkish Empire only in foreign affairs' (in Laqueur and Rubin, 2001: 4). The Hibbat Tsiyon group in the Russian capital of St Petersburg had also called not only for mass Jewish settlement in Palestine but for 'a Jewish government' to be established there as well. Following his essay's publication Pinsker became an inspiration to Hovevei Tsiyon virtually everywhere, to the point where he was chosen to preside over the first gathering of Hibbat Tsiyon societies in and beyond Russia, which met at Kattowitz, Germany (today Katowice, Poland) in November 1884. The Kattowitz Conference created a central coordinating committee for the fledgling movement, headquartered in Odessa with Pinsker as chairman. The so-called Odessa Committee was Hibbat Tsiyon's first permanent organization.

Conflicting visions

Pinsker's emergence as leader did not mean that all Hovevei Tsiyon now saw sovereignty over Palestine as their ultimate goal. On the contrary: although both Pinsker and Lilienblum sought the territorial concentration of Jews – in Palestine or elsewhere, with or without a 'Jewish government' – in order to guarantee all Jews everywhere long-term security in a world of national states by radically changing world Jewry's collective international standing, most Hibbat Tsiyon societies continued to value settlement in Palestine mainly for the reasons Smolenskin had – as a means of relieving the acute economic and physical distress of Russian Jewry alone, without changing the system through which Jews related to others in any fundamental way. In fact, by the time the Kattowitz Conference met, this more limited outlook had pretty much eclipsed Pinsker's political vision, and in his speech to the conference Pinsker himself dismissed it as a dream for the distant future. Meanwhile, he and his fellow delegates agreed, the newly-organized Hibbat Tsiyon movement would have to concentrate on three tasks: propagating the idea that Jews ought to settle Palestine, assisting settlers during their first years in the country and raising funds for these two activities and for land purchase. The work of gaining official Ottoman and European support for mass Jewish migration to Palestine, which *Autoemancipation* had declared a primary necessity and the Bilu had vowed to pursue, was put on the back burner.

The main reason for this development was that by 1884 it had become clear that Ottoman leaders would not agree to any arrangement that gave a 'national' group any special status in the Empire's provinces. Since the eighteenth century Ottoman territorial integrity had been threatened by various combinations of European powers, who had already helped strip the Empire of many of its former holdings in the Balkans and North Africa, sometimes by championing local separatist movements. Thus, when former British MP and Christian mystic Laurence Oliphant (1829–1888) suggested in 1879 (in the wake of Turkey's military defeat by Russia and a peace settlement that transferred significant Ottoman holdings to Russia, Austria-Hungary and Britain) that settling masses of Russian Jews along and to the east of the Jordan River would earn the Ottomans both a buffer against further Russian territorial designs and the gratitude of wealthy Jewish financiers like the Rothschilds, most Ottoman officials feared a Trojan horse. Shortly after his negotiations concluded unsuccessfully, in November 1881, the Ottoman government announced that Jewish immigrants would be allowed to settle only 'as scattered groups throughout the . . . Empire, excluding Palestine', provided they became Ottoman subjects (in Mandel, 1976: 2). True, the policy didn't stick, mainly because it violated treaty obligations with Russia and other European countries and because local Ottoman officials were often unable or unwilling to enforce it. Also, for purposes of this decree the Ottomans defined 'Palestine' as the immediate environs of Jerusalem alone. Still, Ottoman wariness was widely reported in European Jewish newspapers from mid-1882 on, and Hovevei Tsiyon understood that speaking openly about eventual political designs on the country was ill-advised.

But if so, why did they make Pinsker their leader? Probably his greatest attraction was his biography. Unlike the other senior figures in Hibbat Tsiyon, most of whom came from provincial backgrounds, had only a traditional Jewish religious education

41

and had acquired knowledge of European languages, learning and manners on their own, Pinsker moved easily among the Central European Jewish middle class, where other Hibbat Tsiyon leaders felt awkward. Where others used Hebrew or Russian to spread their message, Pinsker wrote *Autoemancipation* in German. He thus seemed a good front man for the new movement, a bridge to wealthier German Jews whose potential as a source of funds was significantly greater than what appeared available in Eastern Europe.

Indeed, funds were Hibbat Tsiyon's Achilles heel. Contrary to Smolenskin's expectation, moving Jews to agricultural settlements in Palestine turned out to be much more expensive than helping them migrate to more developed, labour-seeking countries, mainly because of the need to purchase land, build infrastructure and train the new farmers. As a result, the major Jewish philanthropic organizations in Western Europe and the United States, whom both Smolenskin and Pinsker expected would support their projects, were reluctant to do so. Individual wealthy supporters needed to be found, but even with Pinsker leading the way the Odessa Committee proved woefully unsuccessful: between 1884 and 1890 it was able to invest only a quarter of a million francs (about $50,000 then, with purchasing power of $1.2 million in 2006) in Palestine, much less than what immigrants from Romania had spent to start up their two settlements – Rosh Pinna and Samarin (today Zichron Yaakov) – in 1882. Settlers thus needed to find support on their own; the Hibbat Tsiyon organization couldn't help them.

They soon found a patron in the French Baron Edmond de Rothschild (1845–1934), scion of the great Jewish banking family, who envisioned the settlements as places to experiment with new models of farming and colonization – matters in which he took both an economic and a philanthropic interest. By 1890 Rothschild managed nine out of the thirteen existing settlements, spending over 8 million francs on their maintenance. But that amount, impressive as it was, did not permit much growth. In fact, his agenda chimed neither with the settlers' nor with that of Hibbat Tsiyon; in 1887 colonists revolted against his administration, and shortly thereafter he scaled back his support. Thus at the end of the decade Palestine appeared a likely answer neither to the economic problems of East European Jews nor to their broader security concerns. As Asher Ginzberg, a member of the Odessa Committee who visited the country in 1891, noted ruefully, 'the partisans of Palestine have admitted to their opponents that Palestine is not capable at present of receiving the masses of our people who are leaving the country of their birth' (1947: 23).

Ahad Ha'am (Asher Ginzberg, 1856–1927)

A native of the Ukrainian town of Skvyra, near Kiev (Kyiv), son of a wealthy local merchant, the future 'Ahad Ha'am' (literally 'one of the people', a play on Genesis 26:10 as interpreted by the medieval Jewish exegete Rashi) studied the typical curriculum of traditional Jewish religious texts while teaching himself modern languages, literature and philosophy. After moving to Odessa in 1884 he became active in Hibbat Tsiyon circles, although he criticized the organization for despatching settlers to Palestine who lacked the spiritual fortitude and commitment to national ideas that would enable them to endure the country's hardships. In 1889 he helped organize a society called *B'nei Moshe* (Children of Moses), made up of a handful of young intellectuals who styled themselves purveyors of the national cultural values upon which success of the Hibbat Tsiyon project depended. Over the next four decades he disseminated his ideas in over one hundred essays, written with a distinctive deductive logic and clarity of expression that established him as the foremost Hebrew expository stylist of his day. He expressed a similar critical stance towards the ZO under Herzl's leadership, seeking to turn the movement from a 'political' to a 'cultural' direction.

In 1907 he took a job in London, where he served as mentor to the group of Zionists whose contacts with the British government helped to produce the Balfour Declaration in 1917. In 1922 he moved to Tel Aviv, where the street on which he lived today bears his name.

Ginzberg was not prepared to give up, though; despite all he clung to the prospect of Palestine as 'a place under the sun . . . where even a Jew can hold his head high as a human being, where he can earn his bread from the land by the sweat of his brow, and where he can create the conditions of his own life for himself, in the spirit of his people' (23). But unlike Lilienblum and Pinsker, he did not value the country for its potential contribution to Jews' collective safety, for he expected that only a small portion of the world's Jews would ever be able to support themselves there. Two years earlier, in the article that launched his journalistic career under the pseudonym 'Ahad Ha'am', he had warned that settlement would succeed only if undertaken by a select few, willing to sacrifice their personal welfare for the benefit of future generations. Now, in an essay following Pinsker's death in 1891, he asserted that that select few would create 'a safe haven' not 'for the Jews' but only 'for Jewishness' – the set of cultural attributes that could justify recognition of Jews throughout the world as a nation among nations. He was concerned that the growing integration of Jews outside of Eastern Europe into the societies and cultures of the states that had granted them citizenship would thwart recognition. In order to be a true nation, he held, Jews in all countries needed to be united by something more than religion, but the more Jews in Britain, France or Germany became Britons, Frenchmen or Germans like all others, the weaker such worldwide ties became, and the less the Jewish masses in Eastern Europe (who *did* possess clear national features and needed to claim national status in order to defend their collective needs in the political arena) could make the claim stick. To his mind, Palestine was the optimal focus around which to build a new Jewish national identity. Young Jews already in the country could, he thought, join with a small number of carefully chosen immigrants to form model self-sustaining farming communities that would break negative stereotypes of the Jewish merchant and allow Jews the world over to take pride. Those Jews would also speak Hebrew – the quintessential Jewish language – as their native tongue and produce a modern secular Hebrew literature. Because Hebrew enjoyed a certain cachet among Christians as the language of the Bible, Europeans would take positive notice, while Jews throughout Europe and beyond would learn the language and use it as a vehicle for expressing a Jewish national ethos. Thus, in what eventually came to be called the 'Ahad-Ha'amist' version of Zionism, Palestine would become the Jewish 'national cultural center', displaying to the world a 'true miniature of the Jewish people as it ought to be' (47).

But under prevailing conditions in the early 1890s, even this limited vision had little chance of success. True, in 1891 things were looking up slightly for Hibbat Tsiyon. The organization gained legal recognition in Russia, helping it to raise a bit more capital; those increased funds and a small upturn in immigration helped establish nine new settlements. The movement also acquired a new name: Viennese publicist Nathan Birnbaum dubbed the activities of the Hovevei Tsiyon 'Zionism'. The underlying problems remained, however; Ahad Ha'am himself understood that 'the only path left to us is to turn to our brothers in the West . . . who know what it takes to get things done and who possess all of the necessary means' (29). But prospects of recruiting those western brothers, who, successfully integrating into citizen-based states, felt little urgency to realize any of the various Hibbat Tsiyon visions, were slim.

Indeed, but for intervention from an unexpected direction, the young Zionist movement, like most other projects to build Jewish farming colonies in far-flung parts of the globe, would likely have died on the vine.

'The prophet of the Jewish state'

In February 1896 a Hungarian-born Jewish playwright and journalist from Vienna, Tivadar (Theodor) Herzl, published an 80-page German-language pamphlet that Zionists would soon recognize as their movement's foundational text. Titled *The Jewish State*, its central postulate resembled the one Pinsker had raised fourteen years earlier: 'Let sovereignty be granted us [Jews] over a portion of the globe adequate to meet our rightful national requirements' (in Hertzberg, 1997: 220). Unlike Pinsker, however, Herzl claimed to have discovered the 'motive force' that, 'if properly harnessed', would make a sovereign Jewish national state a reality. The clarity and conviction with which he explained how Zionists could accomplish their goal, together with a biography even less common among them than Pinsker's, catapulted him to leadership. Israel's Declaration of Independence enshrined him as 'the prophet of the Jewish state'.

Theodor Herzl (1860–1904)

Son of a well-to-do haberdasher from Pest (the eastern sector of Budapest) who was a leader of his city's neolog (liberal) Jewish community, Herzl studied at a Hungarian-language Jewish elementary school that promoted integration into Magyar society. At home he spoke German; later he acquired French and English, but he knew no Yiddish and encountered Hebrew only as a liturgical language. In 1878 his family moved to Vienna, where he took a degree from the university's law faculty six years later.

Herzl soon abandoned law for freelance writing. Between 1884 and 1894 he wrote a dozen plays, only some of which were produced. He earned his living as a journalist, becoming familiar to Viennese readers as an entertaining writer of sketches and feature stories. In 1891 he went to work as Paris correspondent for *Neue Freie Presse*, Vienna's leading liberal newspaper. There he encountered powerful sentiments castigating purported Jewish influence over France's political and cultural life. Those sentiments, which found vociferous expression during the Dreyfus trial, set him thinking about how their force could best be blunted. After brief advocacy of mass conversion, he turned to the ideas he developed in *The Jewish State*.

His pamphlet aroused sufficiently enthusiastic reception to persuade him to devote the bulk of his energies to realizing his plan, even though he had to continue his journalistic work to support his family. To further both ends he wrote a utopian novel, *Altneuland* (Old-New Land, 1902), which described an idyllic life in a future Jewish Palestine for Jews and non-Jews alike. However, the strains of his position impaired his health, leading to his death at age 44.

Herzl was an unlikely candidate for such a role. Before the mid-1890s he had shown little concern for Jewish affairs, and he knew of the travails of the Jewish masses in Eastern Europe only from what he read in European newspapers. His interest began only after he reported from Paris on growing tensions between liberals and monarchists in the Third French Republic, which reached crisis proportions when monarchists exploited the 1894 conviction of Jewish Army Captain Alfred Dreyfus for espionage to skewer the Republic's liberal leaders for allowing a serious security breech. Like most at the time, Herzl did not doubt Dreyfus's guilt; only later did evidence of innocence begin to accumulate. He was shocked, however, by the role that Dreyfus's Jewishness played not only in public hostility towards him but in monarchist propaganda against the regime. Indeed, much of the right-wing press charged that Dreyfus's (supposed) treachery was typical Jewish behaviour, proving that the Republican government was controlled by nefarious Jewish interests. It was the ability of the political right to turn anti-Jewish canards into a powerful force for mass mobilization against the liberal political order Herzl cherished that set him to thinking how that force could be blunted. That was the context in which his *Jewish State* was born.

Herzl refused to attribute the attraction of anti-Jewish slogans to anything Jews themselves habitually said or did. Like Pinsker (whom he had not read), he believed that, because Jews were everywhere a minority, all European societies were historically conditioned to view them as alien. Hostility towards them was thus, in his view, a society's natural reaction to the presence of a foreign body in its midst, a sort of allergic response triggered inevitably once the Jewish allergen reached a certain threshold level. Hence, he reasoned, wherever Jews were present in Europe 'in appreciable numbers', antiliberal forces would always be able to threaten liberal regimes that tolerated their presence. Those regimes and their supporters thus had, in Herzl's view, an interest in reducing the number of Jews in their territories; by doing so, they would rob their political opponents of a powerful weapon. That interest was the 'motive force' he expected would make Jews a sovereign nation. 'The world needs the Jewish State', he wrote; 'therefore it will arise' (in Hertzberg, 1997: 206).

That message made Eastern Europe's foundering Hovevei Tsiyon take notice. They understood that they could not turn any of their various visions into reality without assistance, but the West European Jews with financial means and organizational know-how to whom they looked had not responded to their call. Now a westerner offered them the prospect of aid from a potentially decisive source – the governments of Europe. Those governments, many Hovevei Tsiyon figured after reading *The Jewish State*, would surely force a recalcitrant but weak Ottoman Empire to turn Palestine into the 'sovereign pashalik' that Pinsker had imagined if only someone would explain to them why it was in their interest to do so. Herzl seemed perfectly suited to do the explaining. He was young, handsome and charismatic; his plays and journalistic writing had already won him a non-Jewish audience; he knew how to behave in the social circles in which European diplomats moved; and he spoke fluent German, French and English. No such resource had been available to Zionists before.

But was Herzl really available to them, and would he really foster their aims? Before writing *The Jewish State* he had only the vaguest notion of their activities. Nor did he regard Palestine as the only possible territory for the state. Thus following the pamphlet's appearance several Hibbat Tsiyon societies contacted Herzl to explore whether they might work together. For his part Herzl was delighted with the overtures, for in Western and Central Europe his ideas had encountered strong opposition from a Jewish leadership unwilling to accept his contention that they could never be entirely secure in their countries of residence. Like Pinsker, he quickly came to focus on Palestine because Jews interested in settling Palestine were the ones who showed the most interest in his idea.

Though many Hibbat Tsiyon leaders remained sceptical, they eventually agreed to attend a World Zionist Congress, where all interested in promoting Palestine-centred projects would meet under a single roof, hammer out a programme, present it publicly to the world in the name of the Jewish people as a whole and create the organizational and financial instruments for translating it into reality. In August 1897 the Congress met in Basel, Switzerland, establishing the Zionist Organization and resolving to seek 'a home in Palestine for the Jewish people secured by public law'.

After the Congress, Herzl wrote in his diary, 'At Basel I founded the Jewish state. . . . In five years perhaps, and certainly in fifty years, everyone will perceive it' (Herzl, 1962: 224). Indeed, Herzl was certain that once the Jews of the world announced to the governments of Europe their readiness to cooperate in a scheme to relocate them to an extra-European territory of their own, the governments would make things happen in short order. He was to be disappointed. To be sure, it took only a bit more than fifty years for the State of Israel to come into being. But the road to the Jewish state was hardly as smooth as Herzl imagined.

Even after his appearance, the Zionist movement remained a coalition of disparate groups and constituencies, ideologically fragmented and numerically insignificant. In fact it incorporated three distinct streams – one concerned primarily with settling Palestine, a second with readjusting political relations between Jews and non-Jews, and a third with creating a Jewish 'national' culture – and it was not yet clear that all three could work together productively within a single organization, the Congress's declaration notwithstanding. A realistic observer at the time would thus probably not have given the Zionist project much more chance of success after Herzl joined it than before.

Recommended reading

Three works are basic for studying the early history of Zionism. The first, *The Zionist Idea*, edited by Arthur Hertzberg (Philadelphia: Jewish Publication Society, 1997, originally published 1959), provides biographies and extensive selections from the writings of the major Zionist thinkers and activists (including Smolenskin, Lilienblum, Pinsker, Ahad Ha'am and Herzl), together with an incisive, 100-page introductory essay analysing the origins of various versions of Zionist ideology in Jewish and European history. *A History of Zionism*, by Walter Laqueur (New York: Holt, Rinehart, and Winston, 1972), provides the most comprehensive English-language account of the evolution of the Zionist movement to 1948. The three-volume history by David Vital, published by Oxford University Press (*The Origins of Zionism*, 1975; *Zionism: The Formative Years*, 1982; and *Zionism: The Crucial Phase*, 1987) is far more detailed, but it carries the story through only to 1919.

On the development of Palestine during the Ottoman period, see the collection of articles edited by Gad G. Gilbar, *Ottoman Palestine, 1800–1914: Studies in Economic and Social History* (Leiden: Brill, 1990). Also useful is Arnold Blumberg, *Zion Before Zionism 1838–1880* (Syracuse: Syracuse University Press, 1985). Ottoman attitudes towards Jewish settlement projects in Palestine are discussed in the first chapter of Neville J. Mandel, *The Arabs and Zionism Before World War I* (Berkeley: University of California Press, 1976).

Ahad Ha'am is the subject of an award-winning biography by Steven J. Zipperstein, *Elusive Prophet: Ahad Ha'am and the Origins of Zionism* (Berkeley: University of California Press, 1993). There are at least a dozen biographies of Herzl; the classic is Alex Bein, *Theodore Herzl* (Philadelphia: Jewish Publication Society, 1941). For a concise exposition of Herzl's life and ideas, see Steven Beller, *Herzl* (New York: Grove Weidenfeld, 1991). An abridged English version of Herzl's diaries has been published as *The Diaries of Theodor Herzl*, edited by Marvin Lowenthal (New York: Grosset and Dunlap, 1962). There are no biographies of Smolenskin, Lilienblum or Pinsker in any language, but their ideas are succinctly summarized in Shlomo Avineri, *The Making of Modern Zionism: The Intellectual Origins of the Jewish State* (New York: Basic Books, 1981).

CHAPTER 3

Diplomacy and settlement, 1897–1914

ACTUALLY, HERZL RAN INTO complications even before the Congress met. Persuaded by Hovevei Tsiyon that Palestine was indeed the best place for a Jewish state, he decided to try what Bilu had attempted fourteen years before: 'to beg [the state] of the Sultan himself' (in Laqueur and Rubin, 2001: 5). He got somewhat farther than his predecessors had; thanks to his newspaper connections he gained audiences with several top Ottoman officials, and a digest of his scheme actually made it to the Sultan himself. But the Sultan rejected his overtures out of hand, calling transfer of any part of his empire 'vivisection' (Herzl, 1962: 152).

Herzl had anticipated such resistance. In *The Jewish State* he observed that recent Jewish 'experiments in colonization' had made Ottoman authorities want to 'put a stop to further influx of Jews' (in Hertzberg, 1997: 222). But to his mind the authorities opposed merely the *way* in which earlier settlers had surreptitiously 'infiltrated' the country, not the *principle* that Jews ought to be welcome there. If Jews would only make a forthright declaration of their intent to settle Palestine en masse and claim sovereignty in it, then, Herzl was convinced, the Sultan would negotiate with them seriously, for the Jewish people had much to offer in return. Foremost among their assets, in Herzl's view, were the resources of powerful Jewish financiers like the Rothschilds, who could, if properly motivated, refinance the enormous debt the Ottoman government owed to European banks. Yet when he mentioned that prospect to his interlocutors in Istanbul, they were unimpressed. That was a rejection he did not expect; in his diary he noted, 'For the time being [it] put an end to all my hopes' (Herzl, 1962: 152).

From the Ottoman perspective, the rebuff made perfect sense. The Sultan had spurned a similar suggestion from Laurence Oliphant years before, and nothing had happened in the meantime to make him less suspicious: Russia still posed the greatest threat to Ottoman territorial integrity, and Jewish immigrants coming from Russia hoping to claim Palestine for themselves were easily perceived as agents of an insidious Russian anti-Turkish plot. Moreover, Herzl hadn't obtained the agreement of the Rothschilds (or any other major Jewish banking house) to offer their services in connection with his plan. In fact, Edmond de Rothschild had branded Herzl's venture a threat to his own activities in Palestine. The Ottomans thus had little reason to believe that Herzl could deliver the goods he promised: at the time of his visit to the Ottoman court he represented no one but himself.

In fact, Herzl's decision to convene the Basel Congress had stemmed largely from his need for significant Jewish backing – a need his abortive efforts in Istanbul had thrown into sharp focus. If the great Jewish bankers would not help him, he would 'set the masses in motion by indiscriminate agitation' and enlist 'all the high-minded, stout-hearted, intelligent and educated forces of the Jewish people' to his cause (188, 207). After all, he wrote to one of his English supporters, 'all the Jews [combined] have more money than the Rothschilds' – and, he presumed, more power as well (in de Haas, 1927: 1/153). But in order to unite 'all the Jews' behind him he had to 'establish a forum to which everyone who labours for the Jewish cause can be invited to give an accounting of his efforts' (159). Such was the Congress's stated goal: 'to advance the interests of Zionism through a public, oral exchange of ideas' (168). But creating such a forum meant taking into account others' views about how those interests were best fostered. The young Zionist movement already incorporated diverse opinions about its purpose and methods, and those opinions did not always chime with his own. Thus the Congress, like his trip to Istanbul, brought home to him the need for compromise.

Herzl and the opposition

He had already decided on one compromise before the Congress assembled. Since his return from Istanbul he had ceased to speak of a 'Jewish state' as his goal, substituting 'a principality with its own legislature, army, etc., subject only to [the Sultan's] suzerainty' (Herzl, 1962: 171). In mid-1897 he had even published an assurance that 'there is no question of taking a single province away from the Sultan, only of establishing a home secured by the law of nations for those Jews who cannot survive elsewhere' (in Vital, 1975: 366). The retreat from the maximum aim provoked stormy debate at the Congress. In the end, however, the rather vague ambition of a 'homeland for the Jewish people', not a 'state', anchored the ZO's official manifesto, dubbed the Basel Programme after the city where it was proclaimed.

Another compromise appeared in the means the Basel Programme endorsed to achieve that ambition, including 'colonization of Palestine by Jewish agricultural and industrial workers' and 'fostering Jewish national sentiment and consciousness'. Herzl strongly opposed the settlement practices of Hibbat Tsiyon, arguing that the relocation of European Jews could not proceed quickly enough to remove the wind from right-wing sails unless the Ottoman government consented to mass immigration in advance. Hence he sought suspension of settlement activity until the Ottomans granted the ZO a 'charter' to bring Jews into Palestine as it saw fit. But most Hibbat Tsiyon leaders balked at the suggestion, for it eliminated the possibility that Palestine could help East European Jews right away. They also feared that if they agreed to shelve settlement at Herzl's behest, Rothschild would stop supporting existing Hibbat Tsiyon colonies. The nod to colonization in the Zionist programme acknowledged their concerns.

So did mentioning 'national consciousness'. Though not all Hibbat Tsiyon leaders accepted Ahad Ha'am's notion of a 'national cultural centre' as the chief Zionist goal, they were virtually unanimous in valuing development of a modern Hebrew literature. Many also actively promoted Hebrew as the Jews' principal spoken language – a role it had not played for nearly two millennia. In late nineteenth-century Europe language was considered a fundamental attribute of 'nationhood'. Hence, Zionists reasoned, if a common vernacular, distinct from that of any other 'nation', did not unite all Jews everywhere, the

Jewish claim to 'national' status (already weakened by lack of a common territory) would be sorely crippled. True, Yiddish fulfilled that role for most East European Jews, but Jews from other parts of the world did not speak it. Besides, many Jews and non-Jews alike denigrated it as a corrupt German dialect, unsuited as a vehicle for creating a modern 'national' culture. Herzl commanded neither Yiddish nor Hebrew, and he showed little regard for either. He assumed that Jews in the future Jewish homeland would speak the languages of the countries from which they came, with German as *lingua franca*. Nevertheless, as a sop to the Hebraists he noted the importance of 'fostering Jewish national sentiment' as a Zionist aim (while for over three decades German remained the ZO's primary language).

Such concessions to the Hovevei Tsiyon were necessary, because besides them hardly any Jews flocked to Herzl's banner. On the contrary, when plans for the Zionist Congress were announced, they were met with cries of outrage from Jewish spokesmen worldwide. The Association of German Rabbis issued a public declaration calling the efforts of the 'so-called Zionists . . . antagonistic to the messianic promises of Judaism' and insisting that 'Judaism obliges its followers to serve the country to which they belong' (in Mendes-Flohr and Reinharz, 1995: 539). After the Congress the chief organ of British Jewry, the London *Jewish Chronicle*, likened the gathering to a Hyde Park demonstration and protested that the Zionists represented no Jews but themselves. Indeed, during the ZO's first year of operation it received membership dues from about 65,000 people – around half of 1 per cent of the number of Jews in the world. If Herzl had hoped that the Congress would mobilize masses for the Zionist cause, he could not have been too sanguine about his prospects. In any event he could scarcely afford to ignore the concerns of those most enthusiastic for what he had to offer.

His moves at the Congress gave him much of what he wanted, as the delegates effectively awarded Herzl carte blanche to set the movement's direction as he saw fit. Thus, once the Congress adjourned, he pretty much turned his back on settlement and cultural activity, directing the ZO's full energies towards the international diplomatic arena. His experience in Istanbul had persuaded him that he would most easily gain the 'charter' he sought by marshalling support from the Ottoman Empire's creditors. Germany seemed the most likely prospect, for since the 1880s Germans had invested heavily in Ottoman enterprises, and German military advisers had trained and supplied the Ottoman armed forces. Herzl also had contacts close to the German regime, who eventually secured him a meeting with Kaiser Wilhelm II during the Kaiser's visit to Istanbul and Jerusalem in 1898. At first the German ruler was favourably inclined and actually broached the matter with the Sultan, but when he observed how gravely the Ottoman regime feared a large-scale Jewish presence in Palestine, he dropped all efforts on the Zionists' behalf.

The German setback did not daunt Herzl, for he thought he held an additional card up his sleeve. Earlier in 1898 he had begun to organize the movement's chief financial instrument, the Jewish Colonial Bank, which, he hoped, by selling shares to large numbers of small Jewish investors, would give the movement the wealth that the Rothschilds had declined to provide. Prospects for the bank, together with a new contact in Istanbul, emboldened him again to court the Ottomans directly, this time making it clear that Zionists sought not to separate Palestine from the Empire but only 'a Charter from the Turkish government' to settle European Jews in the country 'under the sovereignty of His Majesty the Sultan' (in Vital, 1982: 108f.). For the next two years he pursued this track with vigour, until in May 1901 the Sultan himself granted him an interview – albeit as a journalist only, not to discuss Zionism. Over the next year Herzl tried different backdoor strategies with Ottoman officials to bring Zionism to the table, all to no avail. The bank proved no help; in fact, shares were sold so slowly that not until 1902 could it begin operation. Furthermore, it seems unlikely that monetary considerations alone would have sufficed to induce the Sultan to turn a part of his realm whose possession brought him great prestige over to a company of highly suspicious Europeans. Paying off the Ottoman debt proved less important to him than preserving his domain – especially the Muslim holy places, for whose protection he was responsible not only as ruler of an empire but as caliph, the deputy of the prophet Muhammad, titular head of Muslims throughout the world. By mid-1902 Herzl finally concluded that only a change in the Turkish regime would enable the movement to proceed.

Thus seven years after its conception, Herzl's Jewish state looked stillborn. Not surprisingly, too, rebellion was brewing in the Zionist ranks, instigated by a group of young Russian Jews who had been studying at universities in Germany and Switzerland. Because they combined a West European education with roots among the East European Jewish masses, these students – ideological heirs of Hibbat Tsiyon – thought themselves better suited to lead the movement than the somewhat distant Herzl, who couldn't speak the masses' languages and showed little sympathy for the culture that most obviously made Jews a nation. Their insistence that that culture provided the primary basis for the Jews' collective claim to national status also brought them close to the position of Ahad Ha'am, who following the 1897 Congress had excoriated what he saw as Herzl's misplaced priorities. Jews, he had continued to insist, did 'not need an independent state, but only the creation in [their] native land of . . . a good-sized settlement of Jews working without hindrance in every branch of civilization, from agriculture and handicrafts to science and literature', which would eventually become 'the centre of the nation', contributing 'to the common stock of humanity . . . a great national culture, the fruit of . . . a people living by the light of its own spirit' (in Hertzberg, 1997: 267). In similar vein the rebels asserted that the ZO's resources would be better used to support settlement and 'cultural work' – a publishing house, schools teaching Zionist ideas, even a Hebrew-language university – than Herzl's ineffective diplomatic manoeuvres. In 1901 they formed the Zionist movement's first political party, the 'Democratic Fraction'; a year later, at the Fifth Zionist Congress, over Herzl's opposition, they pushed through a resolution obligating all Zionists to contribute to 'the education of the Jewish people in a national sense' (in Vital, 1982: 198). That success emboldened them to plan further challenges at the next Congress, scheduled for 1903.

Indeed, the Sixth Zionist Congress witnessed a full-scale revolt against Herzl's leadership. Ironically, though, the mutiny was prompted not by the Democratic Fraction's machinations but by a sudden *success* in the diplomatic arena. Just as his negotiations in Istanbul were falling through, Herzl caught the ear of British Colonial Secretary Joseph Chamberlain. At the time the British government fretted over the mounting pace of immigration (mostly Jewish) from Eastern Europe and sought options for diverting the stream to other locations. In that connection it occurred to Chamberlain, an architect of late Victorian imperial expansion, that Jewish migrants might serve an imperial interest – populating the interior highlands of the East African Protectorate with non-native settlers beholden to Britain, who would help secure the space between the Indian Ocean and the headwaters of the Nile. Accordingly, in April 1903 Chamberlain offered Herzl a tract in the Protectorate for a self-governing Jewish settlement of a million people or more.

For Herzl the offer signalled vindication when he needed it most: almost exactly as he had predicted in *The Jewish State*, a great European power, worried by the social and political tensions that a large influx of Jews into its realm might bring, had granted the Jewish people not complete 'sovereignty over a portion of the globe' but at least a charter for a Jewish homeland in a clearly-defined territory. True, that territory was not the one the ZO had committed itself to pursue. But Herzl's approach held that what Jews needed most was international recognition of their right to settle and govern *some* corner of the world; *which* corner was secondary. Thus he expected that his movement would jump at the British offer to make Jews into a territorial nation.

He was mistaken. When he sprang the offer on an unsuspecting Congress in August 1903, delegates balked. Opponents argued passionately that Zionism involved *more* than giving Jews dominion over territory; it also incorporated social and cultural goals that East Africa (often mistakenly designated Uganda in the debates) could not achieve. Some asserted that the region could support only large plantation agriculture based on slave labour, which contradicted the ideal of transforming Jews into independent smallholders working their own plots. Others insisted that a place where Jews had never lived before could not become a Jewish cultural centre. If East Africa was unlikely to advance these aims, opponents asked rhetorically, why should Jews migrating abroad choose it as their destination instead of the more developed locales with more hospitable climates (like the United States) that were open to them? Underlying such criticism was the long-lurking suspicion that Herzl's alienation from what was most particularly *Jewish* about Jewish national culture would ultimately relegate the Zionist movement to permanent marginality in the Jewish world.

Herzl still had enough clout in the ZO to forestall outright rejection of the British proposal. His death a year later at age 44, however, allowed the opposition to gain the upper hand. In 1905 the Seventh Zionist Congress shelved the matter permanently. Only then did the three principal streams in the Zionist movement – centred respectively about settlement of Palestine, reconstructing political relations between Jews and non-Jews, and creating a secular Jewish culture in Hebrew – come firmly together. However, some of the movement's greatest stalwarts, for whom political reconstruction eclipsed the other two, broke permanently with the Organization over this issue.

A new Zionist *avant-garde*

Herzl's death, the rejection of East Africa and the realization that diplomacy would not yield a charter for Palestine under present circumstances impelled the ZO to reconsider Hibbat Tsiyon-style activity. It did so, though, from a new perspective. The visibility

Herzl had given Zionism outside Eastern Europe had drawn to its banner, among others, a circle of university-trained, mostly German-speaking Jewish natural and social scientists who found in the new Jewish colonies in Palestine a laboratory for experiments in agriculture, social organization and 'productivization'. During the decade before the First World War these academicians rose to prominence in the movement, along with Russian-born veterans of the Democratic Fraction, most of whom also were university educated. Both groups believed that European science could strengthen the hitherto shaky foundations of the Hibbat Tsiyon settlements.

Their hopes were buoyed by renewed Jewish immigration. Spurred largely by a new round of pogroms in Russia, about 8,500 Jews entered Palestine between 1903 and 1907; between 1908 and 1914 another 24,000 joined them. These migrants were dubbed the Second *Aliyah* (a Hebrew word meaning 'ascent', used in the Bible to designate the physical climb up the Judean hills from the surrounding lowlands) to distinguish them from the settlers of the 1880s and 1890s, now named retroactively the First Aliyah. Indeed, there were significant differences between the two groups. The Second Aliyah was younger: three-quarters were under age 25, mostly single. Its motives were predominantly secular: perhaps only a quarter came for traditional religious reasons. And for many the desire for better personal material conditions was accompanied by a determination to improve the collective situation of Jews as a whole.

In part the men and women of the Second Aliyah understood improvement in the same way as the intellectual progenitors of Hibbat Tsiyon had: like Lilienblum they proclaimed settlement in Palestine as their historic right; like Ahad-Ha'am they coupled settlement with development of a new Hebrew 'national' culture. But socialist ideas played a far more important role in their thinking than they had for earlier immigrants. Many – like much of their age cohort, Jewish and non-Jewish, in the Russian Empire – were convinced of the moral and economic superiority of socialism over capitalism. However, following the teachings of the unorthodox Jewish Marxist revolutionary Ber Borochov, they believed that because East European Jews were concentrated in petty production, they could not benefit from a socialist revolution (or even participate in the class struggle) to the same degree as non-Jewish industrial workers, who produced goods more fundamental to economic growth and state power. Hence, they reasoned, in order to equalize conditions with non-Jews, Jews had to create a situation where they were represented in all branches of economic life. Doing so seemed unlikely, however, in an economy where Jews were in the minority; such a situation could come about only if Jews settled together in a territory of their own, where they would perform all essential economic functions for themselves. The young socialists of the Second Aliyah thus viewed themselves as the vanguard of Jewish economic restructuring as much as of cultural revival and even more than of political reconstitution *à la* Herzl.

Ber Borochov (1881–1917)

Growing up in Poltava (today in Ukraine, then part of the Russian Empire), where his father founded a local Hibbat Tsiyon society, Borochov closely followed the activities of the Russian revolutionaries whom the tsarist government exiled to the town during the 1880s and 1890s. These twin influences are evident in his effort to synthesize Zionism and Marxism. He propounded his synthesis in 1905, when a conference of similarly-inclined young Jews met at Poltava to found the *Po'alei Tsiyon* (Workers of Zion) movement, which eventually became the central element in the labour wing of the ZO. Borochov formulated the movement's platform, which became a foundational text for many pioneers of the Second Aliyah. However, his activity attracted the attention of the tsarist police, forcing him to leave the country. He spent the rest of his years working on behalf of his movement in Europe and North America, returning to Russia in 1917 to assist the revolution.

Unlike most Zionists, who championed the Hebrew language, Borochov also envisioned a central role for Yiddish in the new Jewish national culture. He himself wrote pathbreaking studies of the origins of Yiddish and its grammar, helping to lay the groundwork for the academic study of Yiddish language and literature.

The ZO had not encouraged these self-styled *halutsim* (Hebrew for 'pioneers' or '*avant-garde*') to come to Palestine, but it benefitted immeasurably from their activities. On the surface, it seems strange that these two groups – one a champion of the proletariat, the other bourgeois and capitalist – would get along. They were linked, however, by mutual need. Halutsim hoped to begin economic restructuring by making sure that Jews in Palestine grew food for themselves; hence their first goal was to work the land. But they didn't aspire to become independent cultivators like their First Aliyah predecessors; instead they idealized the wage-earning farmhand. However, existing Jewish settlements weren't big enough to give them jobs; only if new farms were established could they satisfy their purpose. Land for such farms was not readily available, though; Hibbat Tsiyon societies still lacked resources, Rothschild had pulled out of the country in 1900 and the agency that had taken over his settlements, the

Jewish Colonization Association, did not expect to expand operations. On the other hand, in 1901, as a concession to Herzl's opponents, the ZO had established a Jewish National Fund (JNF) to purchase real property should it ever enter the Palestine land market. Within two years JNF raised enough capital to launch operations, and with the change in Zionist leadership following Herzl's death it began buying large tracts for cultivation.

The ZO designated JNF lands for what it deemed Jewish public purposes; the lands were not to be sold but leased to Jews who would work them. The Organization needed to be sure, however, that new lessees would be more successful than the First Aliyah settlers, so that the Zionist movement would not have to support them indefinitely. From that perspective, the socialist halutsim seemed promising candidates. Some of them had formed workers' communes, which, by sharing scarce resources among the members, had lowered labour costs significantly. Thanks partly to the communes' efforts, settlements contracting with them to provide labour for their lands began to turn a profit for the first time. Hence when the ZO established its first office in Palestine in 1908, its director, Arthur Ruppin, turned to a group of them to set up an experimental communal farm on territory near the Sea of Galilee that JNF had recently bought. The offer fit both the material needs of the halutsim and their ideological predispositions, and in 1909 a new type of settlement – eventually called a *kibbutz* (literally 'gathering') – was inaugurated. Named Degania, this first kibbutz signalled the formation of a pragmatic alliance that would direct the Zionist enterprise through to the establishment of Israel and beyond – the connection between the bourgeois ZO's land purchases and the labour of socialist halutsim. Among other things that connection overcame many of the difficulties of First Aliyah settlement, helping place the movement's activities in Palestine on a firmer economic footing.

Arthur Ruppin (1876–1943)

Ruppin grew up in Magdeburg, Germany. Forced to leave school to support his impoverished family, he studied on his own, eventually earning admission to the University of Berlin. Later he undertook postgraduate study at the University of Halle, where he earned a doctorate in political science in 1902. The following year he published a prizewinning study, *Darwinismus und Sozialwissenschaft* (Darwinism and Social Science), arguing for replacement of the capitalist ethic of competition with one of cooperation fostered by the state. Personal experiences persuaded him, however, that even if the German state managed to impose such an ethic, German social prejudices would exclude Jews from its purview. He thus saw Zionism as a vehicle for developing a model Jewish society in Palestine.

Ruppin's interest in Palestine led the ZO to commission him to visit the country in 1907 to report on conditions. His report encouraged establishment of the ZO's Palestine Office, which he directed from 1908 to 1943. In this capacity he supervised Zionist-sponsored settlement activities, becoming in effect the movement's master social and economic planner. Mindful of the need for Jewish settlement to benefit Palestine's non-Jews, he concerned himself with ways to improve Arab agriculture. However, his notion of proper Zionist policy towards the Arabs fluctuated between a binational Jewish–Arab state and resettlement of Arab peasants beyond Palestine's borders.

Through his books *Die Juden der Gegenwart* (The Jews of Today, 1904) and *Soziologie der Juden* (Sociology of the Jews, 1930), Ruppin helped lay the foundations for the social scientific study of Jewish life. He inaugurated the study of sociology at the Hebrew University of Jerusalem.

Local opposition

As crucial as the ZO–halutsim alliance was in getting the Zionist project off the ground, it also provoked tensions between Jewish settlers and Palestine's non-Jewish population – tensions that remain vexing a century and more after they first appeared.

To an extent those tensions were inherent in the basic Zionist idea of moving Jews en masse to a territory outside Europe. In perhaps even greater measure, though, they depended upon historical contingencies; neither the ways in which they were expressed nor their intensity were foreordained. Contrary to what is often asserted, Zionists did not think of Palestine as a 'land without people'. True, the English Zionist publicist Israel Zangwill (1864–1926) – who himself preferred East Africa to Palestine – observed in 1901 that fifty years earlier the British social reformer and Christian millenarian Lord Shaftesbury (1801–1885), in a fantasy about restoring the children of Israel to their former home, had referred to the country as 'a land without a people' and to the Jews as 'a people without a land'. Both characterizations figured in later Zionist propaganda. But it was always 'a people', not individual 'people', that Zionists claimed Palestine lacked. That claim was rooted in the virtually universal late nineteenth-century European perception that true 'nations' existed only in Europe and its immediate extensions, like the white settler states of North and South America. Indeed, because at the time 'nation' was almost exclusively a European concept, few groups beyond Europe, including those that populated the Ottoman Empire, spoke of themselves in 'national' terms. The non-Jewish residents of Palestine whom the first Zionist settlers encountered tended at the time to identify themselves more by occupation, village, religion or family ties than as members of a single Palestinian 'nation' or 'people'. Even the idea of an Arab 'nation', encompassing all speakers of Arabic, was only beginning to crystallize at the time, and before the third decade of the twentieth century relatively few residents of Palestine believed that it commanded their loyalty. Hence characterizing Palestine as 'a land without *a* people' did not seem inaccurate to early Zionists, despite their acute awareness that the country was populated by other human beings.

The purported lack of a pre-existing 'nation' in Palestine provided Zionists with part of what they saw as their movement's moral justification. On the premise that only nations were entitled to exercise sovereignty, many Europeans asserted that they could legitimately lay claim to territories other than the ones they inhabited themselves, as long as those territories were not ruled in the name of any indigenous nation. Because in practice hardly any such territories existed outside Europe at the beginning of the twentieth century, political control of the rest of the world appeared to Europeans, Zionists included, to be up for grabs; the international community – meaning at the time, for all intents, the great European powers – was entitled to award territories around the globe (including Palestine) to whomever it wished, the desires of local residents notwithstanding. Most early Zionists, though, did not believe that local residents of Palestine were likely to oppose their plan to turn the country into an internationally-recognized 'home for the Jewish people'. On the contrary, they thought that by injecting capital into the country's economy they would help raise the standard of living of all its inhabitants, making local non-Jews prefer Jewish domination to that of the Ottomans. During his 1891 visit to

Palestine Ahad Ha'am observed that 'the Arab peasants are happy whenever a Hebrew colony is founded nearby, because they earn good wages for their work and get richer every year . . . [and] the big plantation owners are happy to see us too, because we pay them prices beyond their wildest dreams for rocky, sandy land' (Ginzberg, 1947: 26). Until the Second Aliyah, hardly any Zionists doubted his assessment.

On the other hand, Ahad Ha'am warned that 'should the time ever come when our people's life in Palestine develops to the point where it will displace the local residents . . . they will not give up their positions without a fight' (29). That time came once the ZO entered the Palestinian land market, because large-scale Zionist land purchases unwittingly challenged longstanding local ideas about what land ownership meant. Until the mid-nineteenth century, land use and distribution in Palestine were regulated chiefly by custom. If a peasant family habitually worked a plot, the plot was commonly regarded as 'belonging' to it, meaning that the family could use whatever it produced on it as it wished. Traditionally this right was passed from generation to generation; the state tended not to interfere. Beginning in 1858, however, the Ottoman authorities, seeking both to increase revenues and to define property rights more closely, required landowners to register title with the state and to pay taxes on their holdings regularly. Not surprisingly, the prospect of having to pay for the privilege of farming land that had belonged to their families for generations did not appeal to many peasants. Nor did the requirement to identify themselves to state authorities, which, many feared, would make them subject to conscription into the Ottoman army. Peasants thus began to search for ways to circumvent the new regulations.

In this connection some used the services of well-to-do urban merchants or larger landowners, who were often willing to pay peasants' taxes in return for legal title to the plots they worked. Many peasants thus legally became tenants of absentee landlords, even though from their point of view their plots still belonged to them by customary right. For their part, landlords found ways to use the system to their advantage without disturbing the peasants on their land, making the peasants' daily lives fairly stable.

The landlords' calculations changed, however, when the ZO's sudden demand for real estate drove land prices sharply upward. Under those conditions it made better economic sense for landlords to sell to Jewish buyers than to continue to shield tenant farmers. Indeed, nearly 80 per cent of the land acquired by Zionist agencies before the Second World War was purchased from large landowners, most of whom lived outside Palestine. The buyers, though, were not content to leave the tenants alone; they sought the land in order to pursue some of their movement's most fundamental goals, and because they had acquired it legally, they felt entitled to require the tenants to move elsewhere. Not surprisingly, that situation bred resentment among displaced peasants towards both the Jewish purchasers and the (mostly Arab) landowners, much as a person who has long rented a house might well be angered when the landlord sells to someone intending to use it as a principal residence. Peasant anger, however, was not easily mollified by the thought that the new owners were acting within their legal rights. They believed themselves the true owners of the land and the title the buyers had purchased merely a fiction. To their minds, Zionist settlers had no rights in the countryside without their consent.

Tensions were further exacerbated by competition for jobs between halutsim and non-Jews seeking work as agricultural wage labourers. The number of non-Jews looking for work increased as a result of displacements caused by Zionist land purchases. In order to persuade Jewish settlers to hire them instead of (usually less expensive) non-Jewish workers, halutsim appealed to group solidarity, arguing that Jewish farms should be worked as much as possible by Jewish hands. The kibbutz at Degania was founded on this principle, which soon became known as 'Hebrew labour'. In 1911 Ruppin committed the ZO to it, insisting that on lands in Palestine acquired with 'Jewish national capital', Jews receive preference in hiring. Such a policy, he argued, was needed to make sure that future masses of Jewish immigrants, for whom the halutsim were laying the groundwork, would have jobs when they arrived.

Jewish settlers were aware that their real estate and employment practices would injure non-Jewish peasants (although in 1913 Jewish agricultural settlements occupied only about 2 per cent of Palestine's land area, with Jewish workers making up no more than 10 per cent of their labour force). Settlers discussed compensating those who were harmed, and in a few cases evictees received cash payments from Zionist officials. Ruppin even proposed using ZO funds to buy farmland in Syria and Mesopotamia for uprooted Palestinian peasants. Nothing came of his idea, though. Instead, Zionist observers increasingly expressed concern over growing agitation against the movement in Arabic-language newspapers and among Arab political leaders. They also noted that violent clashes between Jews and non-Jews were becoming more frequent and deadly (though still rare): in four years, between 1909 and 1913, sixteen Jewish settlers were killed in attacks by local Arabs, three more than during the twenty-six years from 1882 to 1908. Such developments, though, did not dissuade Zionists from their course. Although by 1913 some Zionist leaders had discerned the beginnings of a movement proclaiming the political prerogatives of an 'Arab nation' in Palestine (against the Zionist contention that Jews were the only 'nation' concerned with the country's political future), most thought local opposition to be rooted primarily in economic competition. They thus believed that if the ZO offered sufficient funds and technical assistance to those they displaced, eventually the local population would realize the benefits that Jewish-led economic development would bring to all the country's residents and welcome Zionist plans for the country. Others asserted that in the long run the Hebrew labour policy would actually mitigate intergroup friction by creating two separate, parallel economies in which Jews and non-Jews would compete only with members of their own group, preventing one community from taking advantage of the other and confining class antagonisms within ethnic boundaries. Still others saw growing local hostility not as a consequence of Zionist land and labour policies but as the same sort of inevitable reaction to Jewish presence above a threshold level of which Herzl had spoken in *The Jewish State* – a reaction that only the success of the Zionist project could render harmless. Whatever their analysis of the origins of local hostility, Zionists of all stripes regarded the creation of a numerically significant, economically self-sufficient Jewish settlement in Palestine to be vital to the well-being of the Jewish people throughout the world, and they were not about to offer the country's non-Jewish inhabitants a veto over their plans.

Indeed, at the time hardly any Zionists believed that they would ever have to do so. According to the European political ethos that informed their movement, the keys to the kingdom they sought lay not with the country's non-Jewish inhabitants but with its Ottoman rulers and the European powers that influenced them. True, since Herzl's death Zionists had made little progress on the diplomatic front. In fact, they had been disappointed: although they had hoped that the parliamentary regime in Istanbul inaugurated by the Young Turk revolution of 1908 would look favourably upon their plans, the new government proved as inhospitable as had the Sultan (though also as ineffective in preventing Jews from entering the country). Nevertheless, Zionists had recently begun to see significant progress in implementing two other planks in their 1897 programme: settlement of Palestine and creating 'national' cultural expressions in Hebrew. By 1914 Palestine's Jewish population approached 80,000 (about a seventh of the country's total), and the balance between the traditional Jewish community and the post-1881, Zionist-oriented one was moving steadily in the latter's favour. The new community had established a network of Hebrew-language schools and cultural institutions, including a technical college where Hebrew was the language of instruction, and plans were underway for a Hebrew university in Jerusalem. Moreover, although still only about 130,000 Jews around the world paid dues to the ZO in 1913, membership had grown sharply in many countries during the previous three years. Such progress, Zionists believed, could only strengthen their political claims in Palestine, to the point where the international community would eventually be compelled to grant them the charter they sought. As the ZO's official newspaper explained in 1913, if

Zionists diligently 'did [their] work' until they 'constitute[d] a real force in the land of [their] hopes', it would be 'impossible to remove [them] from [their] Fatherland' (in Vital, 1987: 85).

Still, Herzl's prediction of a Jewish state by the mid-twentieth century seemed unrealistic even to the most ardent Zionists. Fifteen years after its founding, the ZO was content to concentrate upon settlement and cultural work, leaving resolution of Palestine's political status for the distant future. In 1914, however, Turkey joined the Central Powers (Germany, Austria-Hungary and Bulgaria) in the First World War, and Zionist fortunes took a fateful new turn.

Recommended reading

The ongoing history of Zionist diplomacy during the Herzl era and after is related in the works by Laqueur and Vital mentioned in the Recommended Reading for Chapter 2. On the story of the East Africa proposal and its reception by the ZO, see also Robert G. Weisbord, *African Zion* (Philadelphia: Jewish Publication Society, 1968).

The crucial period of the Second Aliyah is vividly illuminated in Anita Shapira's biography of one of its central figures – *Berl, the Biography of a Socialist Zionist: Berl Katznelson* (New York: Cambridge University Press, 1984). The English abridgement of Abraham Yaari's collection of memoirs from First and Second Aliyah settlers provides a first-hand glimpse of their experience – *The Goodly Heritage* (Jerusalem: Zionist Organization, 1958). A selection of Borochov's essays is combined with an extensive introduction to his thought by Abraham Duker in Ber Borochov, *Nationalism and the Class Struggle* (New York: Poale Zion-Zeire

Zion of America, 1937). Insight into the work and thought of Arthur Ruppin is provided by his *Memoirs, Diaries, Letters* (New York: Herzl Press, 1971). On the involvement of Ruppin and other social scientists in promoting agricultural experiments in Palestine under Zionist auspices, see the fine study by Derek Penslar, *Zionism and Technocracy: The Engineering of Jewish Settlement in Palestine, 1870–1918* (Bloomington: Indiana University Press, 1991).

Zionist land purchasing practices, the origins of the 'Hebrew labour' policy and their effects on Jewish–Arab relations are treated in Gershon Shafir, *Land, Labor, and the Origins of the Israeli–Palestinian Conflict, 1882–1914* (Berkeley: University of California Press, 1996). Yosef Gorny, *Zionism and the Arabs* (Oxford: Clarendon Press, 1987) surveys debates among Zionist thinkers and activists about the roots of Jewish–Arab tensions in Palestine and what to do about them. On the beginning of Arab claims to national identity, see the articles in Rashid Khalidi *et al.* (eds), *The Origins of Arab Nationalism* (New York: Columbia University Press, 1991). In *The Palestinian People: A History* (Cambridge, MA: Harvard University Press, 2003), Baruch Kimmerling and Joel S. Migdal place the origins of a Palestinian Arab national identity significantly earlier than most other scholars. Compare their approach to that of Ann Mosely Lesch's essay, 'The Palestine Arab Nationalist Movement under the Mandate', in *The Politics of Palestinian Nationalism* (Berkeley: University of California Press, 1973), pp. 5–42, which posits a date after the end of the First World War.

CHAPTER 4

Britain as ambivalent patron, 1914–1929

THE TURN OF ZIONIST FORTUNES flowed naturally from the Central Powers' defeat and the liquidation of the Ottoman Empire in its wake. Palestine had a new master: between October 1917 and September 1918 British troops marching from Egypt expelled Turkish forces northward and placed the country under military rule. In April 1920, the victorious Allies, meeting at San Remo, Italy, gave Britain a 'mandate' to govern Palestine until the newly-created League of Nations judged its inhabitants able 'to stand by themselves under the strenuous conditions of the modern world'. Accordingly, on 1 July of that year a civilian British regime was installed to govern the country. When the League of Nations formally ratified the San Remo arrangement in 1922, Britain's right to govern acquired international recognition.

Zionists were thrilled with the new situation. Unlike the Ottomans, who had regarded them with suspicion and set obstacles (however ineffective) in their path, the British government endorsed the Zionist cause. Three years earlier, in November

1917, Foreign Minister Arthur James Balfour (1848–1930) had announced publicly that

His Majesty's Government view with favour the establishment in Palestine of a national home for the Jewish people, and will use their best endeavours to facilitate the achievement of this object, it being clearly understood that nothing shall be done which may prejudice the civil and religious rights of existing non-Jewish communities in Palestine, or the rights and political status enjoyed by Jews in any other country.

This brief statement, subsequently dubbed the Balfour Declaration, was affirmed by the powers at San Remo, who instructed Britain to use its mandate to put the declaration into effect. The official mandate agreement endorsed by the League of Nations stipulated that Britain 'shall be responsible for placing the country under such political, administrative, and economic conditions as will secure the establishment of the Jewish national home', noting that 'recognition has thereby been given to the historical connexion of the Jewish people with Palestine and to the grounds for reconstituting their national home in that country'. For Zionists the meaning of these developments was clear: British rule in Palestine was to serve but one purpose – to help them make their programme a reality. Herzl's elusive 'charter', it seemed, had at long last arrived.

Zionist ranks swelled as a result: by 1921 ZO membership exceeded 750,000, six times the prewar count. Jews throughout the world appeared swept up in what one observer called 'the expectation of imminent redemption' (Weizmann, 1966: 211). In several European cities Zionist offices reported tens of thousands of applications for immediate migration, prompting a

Polish Zionist leader to predict that within two years Jews would constitute a majority in Palestine, obligating Britain to place the government in their hands. Where on the eve of the war Zionists dared hope at most to become sufficiently strong to avoid removal from their settlements, in its aftermath they contemplated a new status as Palestine's dominant force.

As it turned out, the path to success was neither short nor straight. Zionists soon discovered that they had misapprehended not only British intentions but also their own capacity to turn the postwar political situation to their advantage. For the next quarter century they would search for the best way to overcome the consequences of that error.

Britain and the Middle East

Zionists attributed Britain's support for their movement to two considerations – the congruence of their programme with British strategic interests and Britain's agreement that Zionist demands were right and just. Yet although both considerations undoubtedly occurred to the British policymakers who sought and accepted the mandate to help create a Jewish national home, other ideas and pressures impinged upon their thinking simultaneously, complicating both the political and the moral calculus that shaped their government's policies towards Palestine and the Zionist movement.

Britain's Palestine policies reflected worldwide uncertainty at the end of the First World War about how the prewar territories of the Ottoman Empire (including part or all of the present-day states of Turkey, Syria, Lebanon, Israel, Jordan, Iraq, Kuwait, Saudi Arabia and Yemen) would be governed in the future.

Britain was vitally concerned with this question, because the key supply routes to India (the 'crown jewel' of the British Empire) passed through the Middle East. In 1918, with its troops or allies in control of most of the area between the Mediterranean Sea and the Persian Gulf, Britain was in a strong position to influence the region's political destiny. However, France also had strong commercial interests in the eastern Mediterranean and had long asserted a duty to protect the minority Christian communities in that area. As a result, its leaders were not about to give Britain a free hand. During the war France had used its position as Britain's chief ally to win British assent to divide the historic Fertile Crescent between the two countries. But once British forces captured the region with little French assistance, British policymakers saw an opportunity to modify the terms of division to their country's advantage.

One of the areas in which they sought modification was Palestine. According to the wartime understanding (the so-called Sykes–Picot Agreement), the entire area extending southward along the Mediterranean coast from Haifa to Egypt and eastward to the Jordan River and the Dead Sea was to be placed under an international administration, whose character was to be determined in future negotiations. This arrangement left most British leaders dissatisfied, but because the Holy Land was an area where several countries had long claimed an interest on religious grounds, they required a stronger moral basis than conquest alone to legitimize the exclusive British control they desired. Promising to restore the long-suffering children of Israel to their ancient home seemed to offer precisely such a moral justification, one that would resonate throughout the Christian world, making Britain's deviation from a prior commitment seem like

an altruistic atonement for a historic wrong. Such, at least, was
the public case that Balfour made in 1922 for the declaration that
bore his name:

*Surely it is in order that we may send a message to every land where
the Jewish race has been scattered . . . that Christendom is not . . .
unmindful of the service [the Jews] have rendered to the great religions
of the world . . . and that we desire to the best of our ability to give
them that opportunity of developing, in peace and quietness under
British rule, those great gifts which hitherto they have been compelled to
bring to fruition in countries that know not their language and belong
not to their race.* (in Sykes, 1965: 14–15)

Balfour was not entirely disingenuous: he and several other key
British political figures, including wartime prime minister David
Lloyd George (1863–1945), were heirs to an Old Testament-
based Protestant tradition that fired their imaginations with
visions of Judah's ancient glory. The thought that by pursuing
Britain's global interests they could help restore that glory surely
buttressed their affinity for the idea of a Jewish 'national home'.
But the idea's attractiveness was also rooted in more immediate
motives as well, including the thought that such a home could
offer asylum to several hundred thousand potential East European Jewish war refugees, many of whom might otherwise seek
accommodation in Britain itself.

However, by the time the mandate was ratified in 1922, the
refugee situation appeared far less urgent, and the Balfour
Declaration had already achieved its primary strategic purpose –
gaining international acquiescence to Britain's exclusive hege-
mony in Palestine. Thus after that time it was no longer clear
to at least some British policymakers how the international

obligation their government had undertaken to facilitate creation of a Jewish 'national home' in Palestine continued to advance their country's welfare.

Indeed, events in the Middle East from the end of the First World War increasingly gave British leaders pause to wonder whether ongoing identification with the Zionist cause was wise. No sooner had the British army taken control of the area than local non-Jewish spokesmen began protesting measures they feared would give Jews a significant share in Palestine's governance. Coalitions calling themselves Muslim-Christian Associations reminded army officials that before Britain had entered into league with the Zionists it had looked to another client to promote its Middle Eastern war aims – Hussein ibn Ali (1854–1931), an Istanbul-born descendant of the Prophet Muhammad, whom the Ottoman government had appointed emir (prince) of the Muslim holy city of Mecca in 1908. In July 1915 Hussein, piqued after learning that the Ottomans planned to depose him, had offered Britain a military alliance, promising to induce residents of the mostly Arabic-speaking Ottoman provinces (including soldiers in the Ottoman army) to revolt in return for British recognition of 'the independence of the Arab countries', which included, by his definition, the entire stretch of land from the Mediterranean Sea in the west to the Persian Gulf in the east and from the Taurus Mountains in the north to the Arabian Sea in the south. Additionally he pledged that the future 'Arab government' of this vast territory, which he would head, would 'grant Great Britain preference in all economic enterprises in the Arab countries'. His interlocutor, Sir Henry McMahon (1862–1949), British High Commissioner in Egypt, had encouraged the revolt, sending a young officer, Captain T. E. Lawrence ('Lawrence of

Arabia', 1888–1935), to coordinate strategy; but he had also expressed reservations over Hussein's territorial demands, so that a formal alliance was never concluded. Nevertheless, beginning in June 1916 about 5,000 troops, mostly Bedouin tribesmen under the command of Hussein's youngest son, Feisal (1883–1933), raided Ottoman installations, drove Turkish forces from the Red Sea port of Aqaba, and provided intelligence during the British advance on Palestine. The Muslim-Christian societies argued that even in the absence of a written treaty the correspondence between Hussein and McMahon constituted an agreement, and that by accepting Hussein's military support Britain had committed itself to turn the predominantly Arabic-speaking former Ottoman regions into an 'Arab state'.

By speaking of an 'Arab state', the Muslim-Christian Associations introduced a powerful new element into discussions of the Middle East's future. Like that of a 'Jewish state', the concept echoed the European notion that sovereign political entities were legitimately constituted by pre-existing 'nations'. Indeed, the idea that speakers of Arabic comprised a 'nation' in the European sense and that their 'national' status entitled them to collective sovereignty emerged as a significant political force in the Middle East at the close of the First World War. The label 'Muslim-Christian Associations' reinforced this idea: it intimated that whereas under Ottoman rule religion had been a dominant factor in fixing community loyalties (so that Arabic-speaking Muslims might identify more with Turkish-speaking Muslims than with Arabic-speaking Christians), now affinities based upon language and ethnicity trumped old religious divisions, giving all Arabic speakers not only a uniform national identity but a common claim to a state 'of their own'. The

Muslim-Christian Associations thus expected Britain – which towards the end of the war, following the American lead, had professed allegiance to the principle of 'national self-determination' – to help establish an 'Arab state' wherever Arabic speakers comprised a majority of the population, not only as a reward for Hussein's faithful wartime service but because it was just and proper to do so. By voicing their expectation they rejected what had been the unspoken assumption in Britain's negotiations with Hussein, France and the Zionists alike – that the European powers, and they alone, were entitled to determine the region's political future as they saw fit. They also implicitly challenged the Zionist assertion that the Jewish people was the only one that claimed title to Palestine on 'national' grounds.

To be sure, the Muslim-Christian Associations identified themselves at first as part of a region-wide 'Arab nation', not a local 'Palestinian' one. In fact, in mid-1919 they joined with like-minded societies, centred mainly in Damascus, in a General Syrian Congress, which demanded 'full and absolute political independence' for two loosely-defined areas: 'Syria' (encompassing present-day Syria, Lebanon, Israel and Jordan, together with the western part of today's Iraq, up to the Euphrates River) and 'Iraq' (at the time the Arabic designation for the lowlands between Baghdad and Basra). The former was to be ruled by Hussein's son Feisal, the latter (as decided during a second Congress in March 1920) by Feisal's brother Abdallah (1882–1951). Nevertheless, envisioning that Palestine (which under Ottoman rule had never been a distinct political unit and still had no clearly-defined borders) would become part of an independent Greater Syria, both Congresses explicitly rejected 'the claims of the Zionists for the establishment of a Jewish commonwealth in that part of southern Syria . . . known as Palestine' and opposed 'Jewish immigration into any part of the country'.

The Congresses' resolutions did not disconcert London terribly. Even if the British government acknowledged both the principle of self-determination and the existence of an Arab nation, most of its members believed their commitment to the Zionists rested on firm moral grounds. They accepted the Zionist argument that Palestine 'belonged' not only to the 65,000-odd Jews who lived there in 1919 but to the entire Jewish 'nation' of 13 million, whose needs, as Balfour put it, were 'of far profounder import than the desires and prejudices of the 700,000 Arabs who now inhabit that ancient land' (in Sykes, 1965: 13). The political aspirations of those Arabs, they intimated, would be satisfied along with those of the rest of the Arab nation with which they identified – a nation slated for eventual independence in the remaining Arabic-speaking former Ottoman territories following an interval of French or British tutelage. In any case, from their perspective Britain's strategic interests had to remain their first consideration, Arab national claims (or Jewish ones) notwithstanding. Before the League of Nations formally ratified the San Remo arrangements, those interests still appeared to most British policymakers to coincide with the Balfour Declaration, if only as a demonstration to the international community that Britain could be trusted to honour its global commitments.

Arab leaders in Palestine, however, were determined to change the British calculations. Thus, simultaneously with the Congresses, Muslim-Christian Associations in Jerusalem, Jaffa and other Palestinian cities organized mass demonstrations against turning Palestine into a political entity separate from

Syria in which Jews played a dominant role. Following the second Congress some demonstrations turned violent. A three-day riot in Jerusalem in April 1920, in which a mob attacked Jewish neighbourhoods, killing six, brought home to London what some officials of the British military administration had warned from the outset of their mission – that 'the Palestinians desire their country for themselves and will resist any general immigration of Jews . . . by every means in their power including active hostilities' (in McTague, 1978: 58). As a result, while continuing to pursue the pro-Zionist mandate that the San Remo Conference proclaimed only three weeks after the Jerusalem disturbances, British leaders also began to think seriously about how to forestall such hostile behaviour.

The strategy they developed depended upon a minimalist interpretation of what a 'Jewish national home' implied in practice. The phrase, which recalled the 'homeland for the Jewish people' that the ZO defined as Zionism's aim in 1897, was originally proposed by Zionist spokesmen during the negotiations leading up to the Balfour Declaration precisely because of its imprecision: it bridged the gap between the maximal Zionist goal of a 'Jewish state' and the 'asylum' or 'refuge' that Foreign Office negotiators initially had in mind. It subsequently entered the San Remo protocols even though understandings of its meaning varied widely. Most Zionists appear to have accepted that the mandate had 'not promised us a state but . . . an autonomous organization in Palestine for the Jewish people that may one day develop and assume a leading role' in the country (Gruenbaum, 1951: 110), although they anticipated that should Jews form a majority of the population, Britain would declare Palestine a self-governing 'Jewish Commonwealth'. They also expected that Britain would allow Jews to enter the country freely and grant them first claim upon public resources, interpreting the mandate's provision that 'the Administration of Palestine . . . shall facilitate Jewish immigration . . . and shall encourage . . . close settlement of Jews on the land' to mean that Britain would help defray the cost of settling Jewish immigrants in the country and would make public lands available to the ZO. In contrast, both the British civil administration in Palestine, which began operations in July 1920 under the supervision of High Commissioner Herbert Samuel (1870–1963), and the Colonial Office under Secretary Winston Churchill (1874–1965), who took up his position in February 1921, offered a more limited reading. Samuel explicitly defined his task as 'to administer the country, not for the benefit of one section of the population only, but for all; not commissioned by the Zionists but in the name of the king' (in Wasserstein, 1976: 763). Specifically, he insisted that British funds not be used to aid Jewish immigrants or subsidize Zionist development projects, and he promulgated a land ordinance that nominally encumbered Zionist purchases in the hope of minimizing peasant displacement. He also proposed establishing an advisory Legislative Council in which Arabs would hold 80 per cent of the elected seats (with the mandatory administration retaining veto power over its acts), and he implored the Zionists publicly to renounce a 'Jewish state' as their ultimate goal. None of these measures, he insisted, was incompatible with British obligations under the mandate. True, he announced, 'for the time being there will be no Jewish state, [but] there will be restricted immigration . . . [and] cautious colonisation, [and] in fifty years there may be a Jewish majority . . . [with] the Government predominantly Jewish' (774).

Churchill's vision was even more circumscribed. In June 1922, in an 'Official Statement of British Policy in Palestine', he noted that 'in the last two or three generations the Jews have recreated in Palestine a community . . . [with] political, religious, and social organizations, its own language, its own customs, its own life'. This community, he declared, already displayed ' "national" characteristics'. Thus, he continued, 'when it is asked what is meant by the development of the Jewish National Home in Palestine, it is . . . the further development of the existing Jewish community'. He avowed that immigration would be one means to such further development; however, he insisted, 'immigration cannot be so great . . . as to exceed . . . the economic absorptive capacity of the country'. Immigrants could not 'be a burden upon the people of Palestine as a whole' and 'should not deprive any section of the present population of their employment'. In his interpretation, Britain's sole obligation under the mandate was to guarantee that whatever permanent regime arose in Palestine following the mandate's termination recognized that the country's Jewish community was 'in Palestine as of right and not on suffrance'; the thought that His Majesty's Government had committed itself to make Palestine 'as Jewish as England is English' was unfounded.

Churchill's pronouncement contained an additional nod to Arab apprehensions: 'The terms of the [Balfour] Declaration do not contemplate that Palestine as a whole should be converted into a Jewish National Home, but that such a Home should be founded *in Palestine*.' Thus British policy, Churchill proclaimed, did not aim at 'the disappearance or subordination of the Arabic population, language, or culture in Palestine'. Indeed, over a year earlier he had moved drastically to restrict the portion of

Palestine to which the terms of the Balfour Declaration applied. According to the San Remo protocols, which first translated the broad geographic notions of 'Syria', 'Lebanon', 'Iraq' and 'Palestine' into political units with recognized borders (awarding France a mandate over the first two countries, Britain over the final two), Britain's obligations under the Palestine mandate extended both east and west of the Jordan River, including the territories not only of present-day Israel but of the present-day Kingdom of Jordan as well. However, the Transjordanian areas, inhabited largely by semi-nomads, proved difficult to control, and with British troops in the Middle East spread thin from Egypt to Afghanistan, Churchill looked for a client who could maintain order. He settled upon Abdallah, son of Hussein, promising, among other things, that the region for which he was to be responsible – almost 80 per cent of the mandatory territory – would be off limits to development related to the Jewish national home. Soon 'Transjordan' became a separate British protectorate with Abdallah as emir, with the term 'Palestine' reserved for lands between the Jordan River and the Mediterranean Sea.

The Samuel–Churchill strategy failed to reconcile the Arab leadership of Palestine to the British mandate. Arabs boycotted the elections to the Legislative Council, which never came into being. Their political representation, the Arab Executive, chosen in December 1920 at a congress of Muslim-Christian Associations, steadfastly refused to acknowledge any Zionist claims or desires; it consistently demanded nothing less than renunciation of the Balfour Declaration, cessation of Jewish immigration and land purchases, and immediate establishment of an Arab 'national government' for Palestine. In fact, after 1922 – when

Egypt gained nominal independence, Transjordan became effectively established as an autonomous Arab province and French-controlled Lebanon and Syria began to build local administrations in which Arabs dominated – the Arabs of Palestine increasingly thought of themselves as a distinct 'nation', one whose needs and interests were not necessarily identical with those of Arabs in other countries and whose aspirations for sovereignty could not be satisfied by the existence of other Arab states. Despite all efforts to mitigate them, Palestinian Arab grievances against Britain became the most deeply-felt in all the Arab world.

On the other hand, following the April 1920 disturbances and a second outbreak in May 1921, mob attacks by Arabs upon Jews virtually ceased, as did large-scale demonstrations against the mandatory regime. This development was partly the result of effective police work by the military and paramilitary forces that Britain stationed in the country. Maintaining those forces was expensive, however. Thus, concerned for the high cost of maintaining order, British leaders developed an attitude of watchful waiting. As long as quiet prevailed between the Jewish and Arab communities, they would show as much sympathy for the Zionist project as Churchill's 1922 policy statement allowed. But the possibility that they would need to re-evaluate their commitment to the Zionists should hostilities reach a level that could be suppressed only by increased force was never far from their minds.

Sustaining the Zionist enterprise

Another partial reason for the virtual disappearance of violent Arab protest during the 1920s was a widespread feeling in

Palestine that, for all the boost they had gained from the mandate, the Zionists would prove unable to carry their programme through to completion. In fact, by the middle of the decade Zionist leaders themselves sensed that their movement might well be on the verge of collapse.

Ironically, it was the very upsurge in European Jewish demand for migration to Palestine following the First World War that revealed the movement's weakness. The war, much of which was fought in the areas of densest Jewish settlement, displacing several hundred thousand Jews from their homes, had been followed by a spurt of violence in the ethnically-mixed borderlands of the former Russian and Austro-Hungarian empires vastly more lethal than any that had beset Jews in recent centuries. Between 1918 and 1920 some 60,000 Jews died in pogroms – the greatest concentrated loss of Jewish life until the Nazi Holocaust of the 1940s. Similarly, as late as mid-1921 more than 200,000 Jews who had fled wartime fighting or postwar hostility remained without homes. In the same year the United States, which in the decade before the war had admitted an average of over 100,000 Jewish immigrants each year, enacted an Emergency Quota Act, drastically restricting immigration possibilities, especially from Eastern Europe, even as some of the newly-created nation-based states in that region took measures that placed their Jewish minorities at an economic disadvantage. As a result, hundreds of thousands of East European Jews sought relief from immediate distress, and Palestine appeared to many of them the most readily available place to find it. Yet the prospect of so many immigrants descending upon the country in a brief interval seems to have frightened the Zionist leadership almost as much as it did Arab spokesmen. The mandatory administration's insistence

that no British funds be used to promote Jewish settlement left
the ZO entirely responsible for immigrant welfare, just as it had
been during the Ottoman era. In fact, the administration's first
immigration ordinance required the ZO to guarantee a year's
financial support for all Jews arriving in the country without
independent means. The ZO also had to finance basic services
for Jewish immigrants – not only housing, but also schools and
health care; the administration denied public funds for those
purposes. Yet despite the dramatic postwar rise in the number
of its dues-paying members, the Organization's pockets were
not deep, and wealthy backers were few. From 1920 to 1925 it
was able to spend on average less than £500,000 per year in
Palestine; a campaign to raise £25 million for immigrant settlement over the same interval garnered less than one-tenth that
amount. As a result, the ZO found itself in the paradoxical position of telling Jews looking to escape difficult circumstances
that 'the time has not yet come for large-scale immigration
to Palestine, certainly not large enough to bring relief to the
masses' (in Mendelsohn, 1986: 112). In late 1920 ZO President
Chaim Weizmann indicated that the Organization could handle
only about 1,000 immigrants per month, far fewer than the
16,500 families that Herbert Samuel set as the country's
'economic absorptive capacity' around the same time.

Chaim Weizmann, 1874–1952

Weizmann was the Zionist movement's principal statesman
during the years of the British mandate, the one who brought it
to the threshold of statehood. Growing up in a village near Pinsk
(in present-day Belarus), he studied in German universities before
obtaining a doctorate in chemistry from the University of Geneva

in 1900. During his studies he became involved in a circle of
Russian Jewish students heavily influenced by Ahad Ha'am.
He attended Zionist Congresses beginning in 1898 and became
one of the leaders of the Democratic Fraction.

In 1904 he joined the faculty of the University of Manchester,
moving to London in 1916 to develop his process for synthesizing
acetone, a vital ingredient for Britain's wartime armaments
industry. His chemical research and his friendship with *Manchester
Guardian* editor C. P. Scott brought him into contact with
British political leaders, enabling him to carry on the talks that
culminated in the Balfour Declaration. That coup catapulted him
to the Zionist leadership; in 1920 he was elected ZO president.
In this capacity he developed the doctrine of 'synthetic Zionism',
which assigned equal priority to the movement's diplomatic and
settlement activities and allowed him to forge an alliance with the
growing labour movement. A gaffe in a 1931 newspaper interview
caused him to lose the presidency, but he regained it in 1935,
remaining in office until 1946, when his policy of continued
cooperation with Britain appeared no longer tenable.

In February 1949 Weizmann became Israel's first president.

In retrospect, it appears that the ZO simultaneously under-
estimated and overestimated the country's potential to accommo-
date immigrants. Between 1919 and mid-1923 (the period of the
so-called Third Aliyah) immigration ran to about 650 per month,
a figure that, however modest, raised Palestine's overall Jewish
population by 12–14 per cent per year and the number of Jews
seeking employment by almost 50 per cent annually. Even the
most robust economies are hard pressed to absorb such a rapid
addition to the labour force, let alone the fledgling endeavours of
the halutsim (which had been scaled back significantly during
the war). Indeed, many immigrants might have had to leave soon
after arrival were it not – ironically – for the labour needs of the

mandatory administration's ambitious public works projects. During the early 1920s, the British authorities, chiefly for military-strategic reasons, undertook to improve and expand Palestine's highways, railroads, ports and communications network. In the process it became one of the country's largest employers of Jewish and Arab workers alike. For many Jewish newcomers roadbuilding was their sole means of livelihood, prompting at least one socialist Zionist leader to term Britain's infrastructure investments the movement's 'salvation'.

British pump priming also spurred private investment. In 1921 the British government contracted with Pinhas Rutenberg (1879–1942), an engineer with Zionist ties, to supply electricity throughout most of the country. Within two years Rutenberg raised sufficient capital to launch the Palestine Electric Corporation, which, by harnessing the energy of the Jordan River as it fell to the Dead Sea (420 m below sea level), soon managed to make cheap power widely available. His success encouraged other Jewish entrepreneurs. Noting that building projects created demand for concrete, a Jewish refugee from Soviet Georgia not connected to the Zionist movement opened the Nesher cement factory in 1924. In the same year High Commissioner Samuel helped dedicate the Shemen oil and soap factory, underscoring the government's interest in industrial development. Thanks in no small measure to that interest, the manufacturing sector provided support for nearly 30 per cent of Palestine's Jewish workforce by 1929.

The growth of private industry helped raise Palestine's 'economic absorptive capacity' and paved the way for an unprecedented boom in Jewish immigration: between 1924 and 1926, nearly 60,000 Jews entered the country, raising their proportion of the total population to one-sixth. Still, many Zionist leaders regarded these developments as a mixed blessing. The so-called Fourth Aliyah displayed a different character from the Third: whereas the immigrants of the early 1920s were largely socialist halutsim intent on transforming themselves into workers on the land, those who came during the middle of the decade were mainly lower middle-class Jews, for whom socialism and agricultural labour held little attraction. In fact, many migrated to Palestine less for collective Jewish reasons than for personal ones: the country seemed to offer economic opportunities absent in Eastern Europe, and with the United States enacting even tighter restrictions on immigration in 1924, their choice of destination seemed clear. These immigrants gravitated heavily to the cities, helping Tel Aviv, founded in 1909, increase its population twelvefold (to roughly 45,000) during the 1920s and transform itself from a suburb of Jaffa into Palestinian Jewry's commercial and cultural centre. The ZO, however, continued to adhere to the notion, first articulated during the Second Aliyah, that the Organization's resources were best directed towards projects led by halutsim. The halutsim, for their part, warned that the new arrivals embodied values antithetical to the ethos of labour and national self-sacrifice that the Zionist movement needed to inculcate into the Jewish people if it was to succeed. Building Jewish Palestine with private capital instead of ZO funds would, many Zionist leaders feared, allow the profit motive to direct development instead of what they considered the Jewish people's collective needs.

Palestine's improved economic situation in the mid-1920s meant that the ZO no longer actively tried to dissuade Jews from coming, as it had at the beginning of the decade. But economic and political realities, along with the changing character of the immigrants, forced Zionists once again to confront tensions within their movement and to clarify Zionism's fundamental aims.

Different ends, different means

The tensions of the 1920s came to the fore amidst difficulties in the Zionists' relationships with three groups – Palestinian Arabs, the British administration and world Jewry – none of which behaved as the ZO expected or desired. Their long-term roots, however, lay in unresolved internal conflicts from the movement's formative years. From the outset Zionism had been the activity of a loose coalition of individuals and groups united by a common desire to increase the Jewish population of Palestine for this-worldly, non-messianic purposes but unable to agree about the purposes themselves or the number of Jews required in Palestine to achieve them. Since 1897 these divergent trends had managed to coexist under a single organizational umbrella largely because, absent Herzl's elusive 'charter', the issues that divided them remained largely theoretical. Only once during the Ottoman period, in the East African controversy, was the ZO called upon to take a decision that was likely to bear significant practical consequences for more than a limited number of Jews. In contrast, under the mandate the stakes of ZO actions rose considerably, making the choice among alternative ideas a matter of unprecedented import.

The most basic choice concerned Palestine's political future. Weizmann and the halutsim were inclined to accede to Britain's restrictive conception of the Jewish national home, believing that it was not incompatible with Zionism's most important goals. They gave primacy to Zionism's socio-economic over its political aspect. Indeed, in 1925 David Ben Gurion, an emerging leader of the halutsim, equated the 'national liberation' Zionists sought in Palestine with 'making labour the dominant principle in the life of the people' – a reference to the longstanding Zionist aim of 'productivization' (Ben Gurion, 1974: 231). In theory that aim could be accomplished even if Jews did not form a majority in the country and Palestine never became a 'Jewish Common-wealth'; all that was needed was a government that would permit the ZO to purchase enough land for Jews (in Weizmann's words) to 'live in houses we have built ourselves [and] eat the fruit of the garden we have planted with our own hands' (in Hertzberg, 1997: 577) and allow as many Jews to enter the country as were willing and able to do so. Hence the heads of the socialist–ZO alliance that had spearheaded the Zionist enterprise since the Second Aliyah declined to confront the British authorities over prohibition of Jewish settlement in Transjordan, lack of public funds for Zionist projects, or limitation of Jewish immigration to the country's 'economic absorptive capacity'. In fact, they hoped that by stressing economic over political goals they could mitigate Arab fears. To Arab workers and peasants they offered a vision of two autonomous communities sharing governmental responsibilities and public resources under neutral British supervision, with Jewish investment and immigration sparking economic growth sufficient to sustain a large Jewish population without harming the livelihood of non-Jews.

David Ben Gurion, 1886–1973

The dominant figure in the Zionist labour movement for almost four decades and the State of Israel's chief architect, Ben Gurion was born David Gruen in Ptorísk, near Warsaw; his father was active in Hibbat Tsiyon. Among the founders of Po'alei Tsiyon, he migrated to Palestine in 1906, hoping to become an agricultural labourer. However, his ability with words and organizational skills pushed him to political leadership. In 1913 he represented the Palestinian Po'alei Tsiyon at the Eleventh Zionist Congress. Deported as a suspect enemy alien in 1915, Ben Gurion travelled to New York, where he tried to raise a Jewish legion to help Britain oust Turkey from Palestine. He joined the legion following its creation and returned to Palestine with it in 1918.

In 1920 he took part in the founding conference of Histadrut and served as secretary-general from 1921 to 1935. In 1930 he helped catalyse the formation of a unified labour party, *Mapai*, and became its chairman. In 1933, when Mapai became the largest party in the ZO, Ben Gurion emerged as a leader of the world movement; two years later he was appointed chair of the Jewish Agency Executive, a position second in importance only to that of ZO president. Together he and Weizmann steered the ZO until 1946, when he took over both positions. He also assumed responsibility for the defence of Jewish Palestine and formulated the political and military strategies that culminated in the State of Israel's establishment. When the state was proclaimed, he read its declaration of independence.

Ben Gurion was Israel's first prime minister, serving from 1948 to 1963 (with a hiatus in 1954–1955) No individual has left a greater imprint upon the state's history.

Not all Zionists agreed with their approach, however. Beginning with the Fourth Aliyah powerful voices within the ZO challenged the privileged position the Organization had afforded the halutsim. The most influential challenger was Vladimir Jabotinsky, who disputed both that a socialist proletariat constituted the national home's essential bedrock and that subordinating political to socio-economic goals would make Zionism more palatable to Palestine's Arabs. Jabotinsky held that the Zionist Organization existed for a single purpose – to enhance the physical safety of Jews threatened by the hostility of non-Jews among whom they lived. Reminding his fellow Zionists of Herzl's dictum that such hostility was inexorable wherever Jews were a minority unable to exercise political power on their own behalf, he declared that only when Jews became a majority in Palestine and took over the reins of government would the Zionist movement have accomplished its true mission. Moreover, he insisted, that mission made it imperative that the ZO actively encourage all Jews – capitalists, labourers and shopkeepers alike – who wanted to come to Palestine, no matter what they might contribute to the economic restructuring of the Jewish people or to augmenting the country's 'absorptive capacity'. To his mind, the economic burden of accommodating Jews fleeing hardship in Europe fell first of all upon the mandatory government; that is how he understood the mandate's requirement that Britain 'facilitate Jewish immigration'. If Britain refused to assume that burden, he reasoned, Zionists needed to protest. Accordingly he called upon the ZO officially to reject the Samuel–Churchill interpretation of the mandate, including the separation of Transjordan, and to insist that Britain establish a 'colonizatory regime' – one that would place the full resources of His Majesty's Government at the ZO's disposal for the purpose of creating a Jewish majority and state in Palestine on both sides of the Jordan River.

Vladimir Jabotinsky, 1880–1940

Though he held an official position in the ZO only briefly, Jabotinsky's influence upon Zionist history was profound. The most vocal opponent of Weizmann and Ben Gurion, he formulated an alternative conception of Zionism that obtained renewed prominence when his ideological progeny gained power in Israel.

Born in Odessa to a Russified family, Jabotinsky first achieved renown as a journalist. In 1903 he was co-opted into an Odessa Zionist group eager to enlist his oratorical and essayistic talents. Those talents soon made him a rising star in Russian Zionist circles. In 1906 he helped formulate the so-called Helsingfors Programme of Russian Zionism, which pledged Zionists to concern themselves not only with building Palestine but with securing individual and collective rights for Jews in a reformed Russian Empire.

Jabotinsky gained prominence on the world Zionist stage during the First World War, when he led negotiations with Britain over the Jewish legion. Like Ben Gurion, his great rival, he entered Palestine as a legionnaire, but when he tried to reorganize Jewish self-defence units during the 1920 Jerusalem riots, he was arrested and sentenced to prison. The verdict was soon reversed, and Jabotinsky emerged a Zionist hero. He was immediately elected to the ZO Executive, but quarrels with Weizmann prompted his resignation in 1923.

Subsequently he organized the opposition Revisionist party, which from 1925 to 1935 challenged the Weizmann–Labour alliance for ZO leadership. In 1935 the Revisionists left the ZO, establishing a rival New Zionist Organization; they rejoined only in 1946. From that time the Revisionist spirit of opposition was carried forward mainly by Menachem Begin, who became Israel's prime minister in 1977.

Jabotinsky had no illusions that Arabs would acquiesce to such a regime, even though, like virtually all Zionist spokesmen at the time, he insisted that the future Jewish state would guarantee equality between the Arab and Jewish communities. He was convinced, though, that Arabs would fight *anything* Zionists did in Palestine, for they understood that *any* Zionist success would reduce their dominance in the country. Therefore, he concluded, the Jewish national home could develop only behind an 'iron wall' of combined British and Jewish force. He was certain that Arabs would try to pierce the wall, but he was equally sure that repeated failure to do so would eventually lead them to accept the parity he envisioned. On the other hand, Zionist or British efforts to reassure Arabs by minimizing the scope of the national home would, he thought, merely invite increased Arab resistance.

From the mid-1920s the ZO was rent by increasingly acrimonious clashes between Jabotinsky's supporters (called 'Revisionists') and advocates of the strategy espoused by Weizmann and the halutsim. The latter were always sufficiently strong to deny the Revisionists control of the Organization; Weizmann's 'General Zionists' remained the largest faction until 1931, when they were supplanted by the leading political representative of the halutsim, Ben Gurion's Palestine Workers' Party (*Mapai*). In fact, by the late 1920s the halutsim had managed to co-opt many Fourth Aliyah immigrants into institutions they controlled, especially the General Federation of Jewish Workers in Palestine (*Histadrut*). Histadrut ran the country's largest labour exchange, making it difficult for immigrants seeking jobs to find employment without its assistance. It also established its own commercial and industrial enterprises – most famously a construction company and a marketing cooperative for dairy products – making it simultaneously a labour union and a major employer. Moreover, the health care network, school system, bank, insurance company, newspaper, publishing house and theatre that Histadrut operated with ZO support became for many immigrants, not only halutsim, key vehicles for adjusting to life in new surroundings, socializing them to the values of what came to be known as 'Labour Zionism' and ensuring labour dominance among an increasingly petty-bourgeois Palestinian Jewry. And with Palestine's growing Jewish community supplying an expanding proportion of voters to the Zionist Congress, the labour movement's primacy within the Zionist movement was not seriously threatened.

The strategy of the Weizmann–Labour alliance appeared vindicated in 1927, when an economic downturn replaced the expansion that had sustained the Fourth Aliyah. In that year Jewish immigration fell to 2,713 (down from 33,801 in 1925, the height of the boom), while almost twice as many Jews left the country. The net population loss seemed to many to prove that the Zionist project could safely be entrusted only to the hardiest, most idealistic pioneers, prepared to sacrifice personal material well-being in order to serve on the front lines of the Jewish national endeavour. On the other hand, in 1929 Arab opposition turned violent again, undermining the belief that the Weizmann–Labour approach to the Arabs would eventually bear the desired fruit and lending greater credence to Jabotinsky's notion of the 'iron wall'. Although Jabotinsky and the Revisionists had no chance to gain control of the ZO, the ethos of confrontation and force that they symbolized, as well as the priority they assigned physical security for Jews over economic or cultural development in the hierarchy of Zionist values, increasingly influenced both

General and Labour Zionists from that time forth. Indeed, over the next two decades the ZO would alter its understanding of its aims and adjust its approach to Britain, the Arabs and Jewish immigration several times in response to developments that appeared inconceivable from the relatively calm vantage point of the 1920s. ZO decisions during the 1930s and 1940s would eventually pave the way for the establishment of the State of Israel.

Recommended reading

The fundamental foundational documents of the British administration in Palestine – the Balfour Declaration, the League of Nations Mandate and the Churchill White Paper of 1922 – are available in many documentary collections and scholarly works, including Laqueur and Rubin (2001), and the survey of the Royal Institute for International Affairs (1939). The former also includes part of the text of the Sykes–Picot Agreement. George Antonius, *The Arab Awakening* (New York: Putnam's, 1946) contains the texts of the Hussein–McMahon correspondence and the resolutions of the 1919 General Syrian Congress; it also offers an account of the early development of Arab nationalism and an Arab counter-narrative to Zionist versions of conflicts during the mandate period.

British Middle Eastern strategy during and after the First World War is ably sketched in David Fromkin, *A Peace to End All Peace* (New York: Henry Holt, 1989). A perceptive and readable survey of the British mandate's first decade is Bernard Wasserstein, *The British in Palestine* (Oxford: Basil Blackwell, 1991). Wasserstein's biography of the first high commissioner, *Herbert Samuel: A Political Life* (Oxford: Clarendon Press, 1992), is also useful.

Weizmann, Jabotinsky and Ben Gurion have all been the subject of several biographies each. For Weizmann, the most comprehensive is the two-volume set by Jehuda Reinharz, *Chaim Weizmann: The Making of a Zionist Leader* (New York: Oxford University Press, 1985), which considers his life and career to the beginning of the First World War, and *Chaim Weizmann: The Making of a Statesman* (New York: Oxford University Press, 1993), which carries the story through to 1919. For Weizmann's later career the most useful work is Norman Rose, *Chaim Weizmann* (New York: Viking, 1986). The classic biography of Jabotinsky is Joseph B. Schechtman, *Rebel and Statesman* (New York: Thomas Yoseloff, 1956). Schechtman was a close associate of Jabotinsky. A more recent work, also by a Jabotinsky acolyte, is Shmuel Katz, *Lone Wolf* (New York: Barricade Books, 1995). The two standard Ben Gurion biographies are Michael Bar-Zohar, *Ben Gurion* (New York: Adama Books, 1986), and Shabtai Teveth, *Ben Gurion: The Burning Ground, 1886–1948* (Boston: Houghton Mifflin, 1987).

A useful survey of Zionist-sponsored activity in Palestine during the mandate period is Avraham Revusky, *Jews in Palestine* (New York: Bloch, 1945). Yosef Gorny, *From Rosh Pina and Degania to Demona: A History of Constructive Zionism* (Tel Aviv: MOD, 1989) is a concise introduction to the organization and settlement practices of the labour movement. The clash between Labour Zionist and Revisionist approaches is a central concern in Mitchell Cohen, *Zion and State: Nation, Class, and the Shaping of Modern Israel* (New York: Columbia University Press, 1987). Jacob Shavit, *Jabotinsky and the Revisionist Movement, 1925–1948* (London: Frank Cass, 1988) concentrates on Revisionist social and cultural policy.

CHAPTER 5

From mandate to statehood, 1929–1948

THE RENEWED VIOLENT OPPOSITION from Palestine's Arabs began in August 1929, only nine days after Chaim Weizmann optimistically declared that the first phase of 'Jewish work in Palestine' had been completed and a new one was about to begin (Weizmann, 1937: 2/510). The occasion for Weizmann's optimism was the creation of a new organization, the Jewish Agency for Palestine, accredited to the mandatory government as official representative of the interests of Jews throughout the world in the development of the national home. Before 1929 the ZO had served that function, but despite the dramatic growth in its ranks after the First World War, it could claim to speak for only a minority of world Jewry. The Jewish Agency united ZO members with the many more Jews who felt affinity for the growing Palestinian Jewish community but denied the Zionists' underlying premiss that Jews throughout the world constituted a single nation expressing a collective political will. Louis Marshall (1856–1929), a prominent figure among American Jews who had joined with Weizmann in urging the new Agency's establishment, explained that although he would 'never be a member of the Zionist Organization' and was 'opposed to the creation of a Jewish State', he nevertheless favoured 'the upbuilding of Palestine . . . to afford to such Jews as desire to take up their homes in the land of our fathers an opportunity to do so, and [to create there] a cultural centre to which those may repair who wish to perpetuate our sacred literature, the teachings of our sages and the traditions of Israel' (Marshall, 1957: 763, 775). Non-Zionists like Marshall saw Palestine as a replacement refuge for East European Jews who in earlier decades would have migrated to the countries of Western Europe or North America that now restricted their entry, and they were prepared to offer financial support to Jewish immigration and settlement there. By bringing them together with the ZO under a single organizational roof, Weizmann hoped to cultivate much-needed sources of funding for the economic and cultural projects that he and his Labour Zionist allies had come to see in any case as more important in the short run than the political aspect of the Zionist programme. Indeed, on 14 August, following the Jewish Agency's founding assembly, Marshall and a fellow American non-Zionist, the banker and philanthropist Felix Warburg (1871–1937), assured Weizmann that Jewish Palestine's financial troubles were over. No wonder the ZO president believed his movement had turned a corner.

The rioting that broke out in Jerusalem the following week made the corner seem like the entrance to a blind alley.

Britain reconsiders the mandate

The violence grew out of a dispute between the Jewish and Muslim religious communities concerning the prerogatives of Jewish worshipers at the Western Wall – the remaining rampart of the enclosure that in ancient times had surrounded the Temple, the Jews' central shrine. In the seventh century, long after the Temple had ceased to stand, Muslims erected a set of religious buildings within the enclosure, and the entire compound, including the Western Wall and its adjacent area, became the property of a Muslim religious trust (*waqf*). Jews had generally been able to pray at the Wall, but periodic disagreements arose over specific practices. Tensions became acute in September 1928, when British authorities, responding to Muslim protests, forcibly removed a screen Jews had erected to separate men from women during prayers on the holiest day of their religious year. Though most of the Jews concerned regarded their presence in Jerusalem in traditional religious terms and had little affection for the Zionist programme, Zionist leaders felt responsible for defending the needs and interests of all Jews in the country. Accordingly they took up the religious Jews' cause. In addition to protests to the British government and the League of Nations over what they took to be infringements upon Jewish freedom of worship, they renewed an offer they had made periodically to the waqf since 1918 to purchase the Wall from it. Muslim officials had consistently rejected such proposals, fearing that they were part of a Zionist attempt to acquire control of all waqf holdings, sacred to Jews as well as Muslims. Now those fears led them to construct an extension to a building within the compound that overlooked the Wall, allowing waqf officials to maintain a clear view of Jewish activities below. The construction angered Jews, both for its noise and for the structural changes it appeared to produce in the Wall itself. Zionists appealed to the mandatory authorities to force the waqf to stop work, but following a temporary suspension, building activities resumed in July 1929. In response, followers of Jabotinsky organized mass protests on 14 August, the eve of the annual Jewish memorial for the ancient Temple. Two days later a parallel Muslim body called a counter-demonstration at the Wall, at which Jewish religious objects were burned. The next week an armed mob, responding to unfounded rumours that Jews planned to destroy the principal Muslim shrine in Jerusalem, marched through the city's Jewish neighbourhoods, attacking passersby and setting fire to Jewish-owned shops. Over the next six days the attacks grew in intensity and spread throughout the country; 133 Jews and 116 Arabs died – the latter mainly in clashes with British police trying to restore order.

Herbert Samuel's son Edwin, then a junior official in the mandatory administration, called the conflict over the Wall 'absurd', but British policymakers could not dismiss it so glibly. Their government's support for the Jewish national home, however qualified Zionist leaders may have considered it, had been tempered all along by worries that it might not chime with their country's overall foreign policy interests. As long as relatively few resources were required to maintain order in Palestine, those worries were easily overcome. But the disturbances of 1929 suggested that the Civilian Police Force of 245 Britons, 1,200 Arabs and 213 Jews entrusted with the job (whose size had been drastically reduced in 1926 as a cost-cutting measure) would not suffice if violence continued, while a newly-elected Labour government in London, committed to disarmament, looked askance at the prospect that military forces might be needed to preserve peace east of Suez. The government thus sought to identify what had given rise to the violence in the hope of removing its cause, despatching an investigating commission headed by jurist Sir Walter Shaw (1863–1937) 'to inquire into the immediate causes which led to the recent outbreak' (in Esco, 1947: 2/614).

The Shaw Commission's March 1930 report shook the Zionist camp to its foundations. Although it labelled the previous summer's disturbances an unprovoked attack by Arabs on Jews, it insisted that the attack would not have occurred but for 'the twofold fear of the Arabs that by Jewish immigration and land purchases they may be deprived of their livelihood and in time pass under the political domination of the Jews'. More ominously for Zionist interests, it intimated that that 'twofold fear' was well grounded. The ZO and Histadrut, it charged, had not shown proper regard for Palestine's 'economic absorptive capacity' in encouraging Jewish agricultural settlement, for the country 'cannot support a larger agricultural population than it at present carries'. Indeed, it declared, Zionist land purchases had created 'a landless and discontented class' within the Arab peasantry, whose 'position is now acute'. Defining Britain's principal task in Palestine as 'holding the balance between the two parties in that country', the report urged the government to restate its policy so as to remove any impression of favouritism towards Jews. Small wonder that the report aroused impassioned Zionist protest. Arab spokesmen, on the other hand, reasserted their longstanding demands for immediate cessation of Jewish immigration, prohibition of Jewish land purchases and establishment of Arab majority rule.

The government in London appears to have been well disposed towards the first two demands: in May it temporarily stopped issuing immigration certificates to Jews, and it commissioned an economic adviser, Sir John Hope-Simpson (1868–1961), 'to examine on the spot the questions of immigration, land settlement and development' (2/635). When Hope-Simpson, evidently misreading statistics compiled by the mandatory administration and drastically underestimating the amount of available arable land, inaccurately concluded in October 1930 that nearly 30 per cent of Arab cultivators had been deprived of livelihood from agriculture and blamed the Zionist Hebrew labour policy as principally responsible for this 'constant and increasing source of danger to the country', the government issued a lengthy exposition of its policy, suggesting that more stringent controls on immigration and land purchase were in the offing. That document – the so-called Passfield White Paper, named for Colonial Secretary Lord Passfield (Sidney Webb, 1859–1947) – insisted that the mandate involved 'a double undertaking' to Jews and non-Jews equally and asked Jewish leaders to make 'concessions . . . in regard to the independent and separatist ideals which have been developed in some quarters in connection with the Jewish National Home'. Though protests from the Jewish Agency and many key British political figures induced Prime Minister Ramsay MacDonald (1866–1937) publicly to reassure the ZO in March 1931 that 'His Majesty's Government . . . do not contemplate any stoppage or prohibition of Jewish immigration' and would exercise only 'temporary control' of land transfers, concern spread in Zionist circles that Britain might cease to patronize their project should Palestine appear a trouble spot.

Zionist concern was matched by a renewed sense among Arabs that their best chance of ending further immigration and land purchases by Jews lay in turning Palestine into a strategic burden for the British rulers. That sense was well founded. Beginning in the early 1930s Britain, its economy weakened by the great worldwide economic depression that had begun in 1929, felt continued pressure to reduce military expenditures. At the same time, Japan's incursions into China, the bellicosity of the Nazi regime in Germany and the Italian invasion of Ethiopia raised the spectre of an eventual multi-front war, for which British strategic planners felt their country ill-prepared. The Middle East thus became a region to which those planners urged devoting only the minimum resources needed to hold the Suez Canal. Already in 1932 Britain had relinquished its mandate in Iraq in favour of a treaty of alliance with a sovereign Iraqi regime. Palestine's new High Commissioner, Sir Arthur Wauchope (1874–1947), appointed the same year, envisioned a similar outcome in the territory under his charge. Accordingly he pushed for a Legislative Council with a preponderance of Arab over Jewish delegates to assume increasing responsibilities for self-government.

Arab leaders used this situation to gain London's attention. During the early 1930s various Palestinian Arab groups, finding Wauchope's Legislative Council proposal insufficient, pressed for aggressive defiance of the mandatory administration and boycott of British goods. Some, advocating ongoing violence, carried out armed attacks against Jewish and British targets. In October 1933, Arabs in Palestine's principal cities demonstrated openly against Britain's failure to stop Jewish immigration, which had increased dramatically following the Nazi seizure of power in

Germany, a rightward political turn in Poland and the British authorities' determination that recent economic growth had raised the number of new arrivals the country could afford to take in. By April 1936, after Palestine's Jewish population had swelled to over 380,000 – almost 30 per cent of the country's total – the Palestinian Arab leadership, led by Haj Amin al-Husseini (1895–1974), head of the country's Muslim community, declared a general strike, repeating the longstanding demand that Britain close Palestine's borders to Jewish immigrants, outlaw land transfers from Arabs to Jews and create an Arab-dominated representative council to assume governmental responsibilities. If the demands were not met by 15 May, the leaders warned, Arabs would take up arms against both the Zionists and their British patrons.

Actually, they had already done so: riots in Jaffa on 19 April had left nine Jews dead. In response, the mandatory authorities imposed a curfew and detained Arab agitators under new emergency regulations. Nevertheless, British police forces were initially overwhelmed, even though their numbers had more than doubled since 1930. Riots, sniper shootings, bombings, arson, destruction of trees and crops, and attacks upon infrastructure (including a recently-constructed oil pipeline from Iraq to the port of Haifa) spread throughout the country, creating what the British General Staff called a 'general state of lawlessness' brought on by an Arab population 'in full revolt' (in Townshend, 1988: 923). Twenty-eight British police and military personnel were killed between April and October, along with 80 Jews; 197 Arabs also died in bloody confrontations, chiefly with British soldiers.

Eventually Britain suppressed the uprising, but at a steep price: by 1938 over 17,000 regular army troops and two Royal

Air Force squadrons were redeployed to Palestine, primarily from Egypt. Maintaining order immediately east of Suez thus created an enormous strategic misalignment: it tied down more combat-ready personnel than Britain could have mobilized in either Europe or East Asia had war broken out in one of those theatres, and it actually impaired defence of the canal itself. Small wonder British leaders looked for a more efficient way to make the troubles in Palestine go away.

The geopolitics of the day suggested what that way might be. British planners knew that some Arab leaders in Palestine and elsewhere in the Middle East, including Haj Amin al-Husseini, had made overtures to Germany and Italy, evidently seeking a lever with which to influence Britain's policy in the region. The planners also understood that the Zionist movement could not aspire to such leverage as long as Germany was governed by the Nazi party. Thus the longstanding suspicion that association with the Jewish national home constituted on balance a strategic liability for Britain seemed vindicated. The course was clear: Britain had not only to terminate that association but actively to prepare Palestine for government by an Arab majority. Thus when yet another investigating commission, this one headed by Lord William Wellesley Peel (1867–1937), was summoned not only to determine the causes of the violence but 'to ascertain whether . . . either the Arabs or the Jews have any legitimate grievances' and 'to make recommendation for their removal', Arab leaders anticipated that a fundamental change in British policy was at hand.

And so it was. The change, however, was not what Arab leaders wished. The Peel Commission's report, presented in July 1937, offered a radically new interpretation of Arab–Zionist antagonism. In sharp contrast to the Shaw and Hope-Simpson findings, it held that the clash between the groups had little economic basis: on the contrary, both Arab landowners and peasants were 'better off on the whole than they were in 1920', thanks largely to 'the import of Jewish capital', as well as to improved social services that 'could not have been provided on the existing scale without the revenue obtained from the Jews'. Yet, it stated emphatically, 'such economic advantage . . . as the Arabs have gained from Jewish immigration will decrease if the political breach between the two races continues to widen'. The report had no doubt, moreover, that such would be the case 'if the present Mandate is maintained': 'Arab nationalism', it insisted, 'is as intense a force as Jewish'; 'there can be no question of fusion . . . between Jewish and Arab cultures'; the demands of the two groups 'g[i]ve no hope of compromise'; and neither 'the sincere attempts of the [mandatory] to treat the two races impartially' nor 'the policy of conciliating Arab opposition' have improved relations between them. Indeed, it concluded, enmity between the two groups had become 'so deep-rooted that . . . the only hope of a cure lies in a surgical operation' – partition into two sovereign states, one with a Jewish, the other an Arab majority. 'While neither race can fairly rule all of Palestine', the report explained, 'each . . . might justly rule part of it.'

Actually, the report proposed splitting Palestine into *three* sections. Britain would retain control of areas containing significant Christian holy sites – Jerusalem, Bethlehem, Nazareth and the Sea of Galilee – as well as the Jerusalem–Jaffa corridor (including Palestine's principal railway junction and airfield) and the Red Sea coast. For an unspecified period Britain would also administer four 'mixed' Jewish–Arab towns – Haifa (the country's chief port), Acre, Safed and Tiberias. About 20 per cent of the remaining territory, extending along the coastal plain from present-day Ashdod to the border with Lebanon and inland from the base of Mt Carmel to the Jordan Valley, was designated for a future Jewish state; the rest (including the port at Jaffa) would be attached to Transjordan and ruled by the Emir Abdallah. The report also envisioned eventual resettlement of the estimated 225,000 Arabs inhabiting lands assigned to the Jews, and it called for the Jewish state to pay the new Arab entity compensation for tax revenues Jews would no longer contribute to maintaining the former mandatory territory.

The Peel Commission represented partition as the sole prospect for achieving 'the inestimable boon of peace' between two otherwise irreconcilable national movements that accorded with Britain's commitment to the Jewish national home; the mandate, it concluded, was unworkable. Neither Zionist nor Arab reactions were encouraging, however. In August 1937 the ZO formally rejected the Commission's conclusions, although it authorized its officials 'to enter into negotiations with a view to ascertaining the precise terms . . . for the proposed establishment of a Jewish State' – a hint that it might eventually consider partition in some form (in Galnoor, 1995: 208). No such hint was evident on the Arab side: throughout the Middle East Arab organizations denounced the suggestion that even part of Palestine might be slated for something other than Arab national rule. In September the Arab revolt began again, straining British forces dangerously as the threat of war grew in Europe and the Far East. In late 1938 the British government withdrew support from the partition idea, and after a final abortive effort to broker an Arab–Zionist agreement it announced its intention to terminate the mandate altogether by 1949. A new policy statement, issued by Colonial Secretary Malcolm MacDonald (1901–1981) in May 1939, committed Britain to replace the mandate with a single independent Palestinian state, with the country's Arab and Jewish residents sharing governmental authority 'in such a way that the essential interests of each [group] are preserved'.

The so-called MacDonald White Paper conceived the Jews' 'essential interests' rather differently from how Zionists thought of them, however. Declaring that Jews should be permitted to comprise no more than one-third of Palestine's population whatever the country's economic absorptive capacity, it imposed an immigration quota of 10,000 per year for five years, after which 'no further Jewish immigration will be permitted unless the Arabs of Palestine . . . acquiesce'. It also presaged curtailment of Jewish land purchases. The following February Jews were barred from acquiring any land at all in 63 per cent of the country and severely restricted in another 32 per cent; less than 5 per cent was left available for free Jewish settlement. Growth of the Jewish national home under British patronage had ended.

Zionists rethink fundamentals

British and Arab actions from the Western Wall riots to the MacDonald White Paper, along with an increasingly severe situation for Jews in many parts of Europe brought on by the great depression and the Nazi rise to power, forced Zionists once again to re-evaluate their movement's direction. The course that the movement adopted during the 1920s, the goals and values it articulated, assumed that, for the foreseeable future, Britain, no matter how restrictive its interpretation of its obligations to the

Jewish national home, would supply at least three ingredients essential for realizing its aims, however defined: visas for as many Jewish immigrants as Zionist institutions were prepared to receive, land laws that facilitated Zionist agricultural projects and police protection sufficient to make the country's Jewish residents feel secure in their persons and property. Zionists also theorized that Arab opposition to their activities was confined to small extremist groups unreflective of Palestinian Arab society. The events of the 1930s shattered those beliefs. After the Shaw Commission's report Zionist leaders felt grave concern that the mandatory regime would not long continue to provide any of their requirements. They also understood that their Arab adversaries constituted a broadly-based 'national' movement claiming sovereignty in Palestine according to principles that the international community acknowledged. Where during the 1920s Zionists had assumed that they would have all the time needed to create their ideal national home, after 1929 they feared more and more that time was no longer on their side.

The situation placed the ZO in a quandary. Should it try to persuade Britain to maintain the mandate and the policies it had developed during the previous decade, or should it seek a different government for the country? If the former, what tactics should it employ? If the latter, what alternative to the mandate should it prefer? Meanwhile, in case the mandatory government interfered with Jewish immigration and settlement or failed to protect Jews adequately, how might the Zionist movement marshal its own resources to meet those basic needs?

The mounting difficulties of much of diaspora Jewry added a further complication. The Weizmann–Labour preference for selective immigration and gradual development rested upon the assumption that, no matter how great the distress of Jews abroad, the needs of the Jewish economy in Palestine and the ideological demand for 'productivization' trumped other considerations in shaping Zionist immigration and settlement practices. During the 1930s that principle became increasingly difficult to justify. In 1931 one-third of Poland's 3.2 million Jews lived off support from communal charities, with another third estimated at subsistence level. The situation was not much different among the 750,000 Jews in Romania. Jews in these countries – the largest European Jewish communities outside the Soviet Union – also faced growing abuse and attack from some of their non-Jewish neighbours, as well as mounting hostility from state authorities. The Nazi takeover added Germany's 525,000 Jews to the ranks of those whose material and physical security appeared increasingly precarious. In contrast, Palestine escaped the worst effects of the depression; by 1932 its economy was booming, thanks largely to private capital imported by about 12 per cent of the 9,000 Jewish immigrants who had entered the country during the previous two years. Zionist economic experts thus estimated that Jewish Palestine could take in many more immigrants than had been thought practical only a short while before. By doing so the movement could alleviate acute distress for some (though hardly most) Jews in need of immediate succour. But the neediest potential immigrants were not necessarily the ones that could best contribute to the dominant Zionist vision for Palestinian Jewish society. Zionist leaders understood, moreover, that increased Jewish immigration would arouse concerted Arab opposition. Hence throughout the 1930s Zionist leaders sought to formulate effective policies towards Britain and the Arabs that would help the situation of both diaspora and Palestinian Jewry without abandoning long-range plans for reconstructing the economic and cultural foundations of the Jewish people as a whole.

Not surprisingly, the urgent circumstances lent considerable bitterness to Zionist debates during the decade, both between the Jabotinsky and Weizmann–Labour camps and within them. Weizmann, Ben Gurion and the Mapai leadership argued among themselves about the proper balance between using immigration to 'rescue' diaspora Jews from danger and to 'redeem' Palestine according to the Zionist vision, all the while lobbying Britain for the highest possible immigration quota. They feared, though, that they held a weak hand: any significant increase in Jewish immigration would produce an Arab backlash, which would push Britain closer to the Arab side. Hence, they reasoned, they could neither continue to build the national home nor relieve the plight of Jews abroad without a Zionist–Arab agreement. In this context, between 1931 and 1936, Weizmann and Ben Gurion reiterated the notion of parity – Jews and Arabs should be equally represented in all institutions of Palestine's future government. Chaim Arlosoroff (1899–1933), chairman of the Jewish Agency's Political Department and an architect of the parity idea, presented it as a guarantee that 'ongoing Jewish immigration will threaten no one'; even should Jews comprise a majority of the country's residents, Zionists would not demand a political majority and would not seek to turn Palestine into a 'Jewish state' (in Gorny, 1985: 289). In return they asked Arabs to drop their insistence that Palestine become an 'Arab state'. No doubt they were sufficiently sober to understand that Arab acceptance of the proposal was unlikely; probably they hoped to show Britain a willingness to make concessions in the spirit of the Passfield White Paper, an attitude they hoped would increase the mandatory government's sympathy for their activities and encourage it to resist Arab demands to curtail them. Realistically they expected they might raise Palestine's Jewish population to 40 per cent of the country's total, after which, they thought, they would be sufficiently strong to force Arab leaders to compromise.

To Jabotinsky's Revisionists such talk was anathema. The 'iron wall' doctrine taught that Arabs would reconcile themselves to Zionist plans only once they were persuaded they had no chance to derail them. Hence, Jabotinsky claimed, offering parity before achieving a Jewish majority would only stiffen Arab resistance. Instead, he insisted that the ZO declare its intention to 'turn the entire territory of the Palestine mandate, on both sides of the Jordan, into a Jewish state . . . with a Jewish majority' in the shortest time possible (in Shavit, 1977: 42). He argued further that the British could be induced to support this object once they understood that the Zionists were their natural allies. Jews, he claimed, were the only people in the eastern Mediterranean committed to western notions of progress and good government; therefore only they could help Britain maintain its foothold in the region. If British leaders worried about the costs of backing the Zionists, their worries, he claimed, were misplaced: Palestine's Jews would gladly bear the burden of fighting any Arab uprising with a military force of their own, if only Britain would permit its creation and the ZO redirect its resources towards arms and training.

The ZO rejected Jabotinsky's call to declare a Jewish state its final aim, setting the Revisionists on a course to establish a rival 'New Zionist Organization' in 1935. But virtually all Zionists acknowledged that, failing an agreement with the Arabs, Jews would likely have to employ some measure of force on their own in order to continue the Zionist programme. The principal deployer of that force was to be an organization called *Haganah* (Defence). Initially sponsored by Histadrut as a security force for Jewish settlements, Haganah had gained visibility during the 1929 violence by confronting Arab mobs before British police arrived. From 1931 the Jewish Agency took over funding and supervision; by 1936 Haganah could mobilize about 2,000 trained militiamen. During the 1936 Arab uprising Britain enlisted some 22,000 Jews as supernumerary policemen to guard Jewish neighbourhoods; most of them joined Haganah as well. At first Haganah hesitated before retaliating for attacks during the uprising, confining itself to static defence, but because Arab rebels employed the hit-and-run ambush more than frontal assaults on settlements, it eventually determined to carry the fight to the insurgents. Thus the Zionist movement began to build its own offensive military force, one that could fight in open country and would leave the confines of Jewish settlements to do so.

The emphasis Zionists placed upon military development after 1936 indicated their reluctant recognition that chances of swaying Britain to continue sheltering their project, let alone of reaching agreement with the Arabs, were nil. Their response to the Peel partition proposal was governed by the same realization. Ben Gurion interpreted the proposal as the only realistic alternative to freezing growth of the national home. The majority in the Weizmann–Labour camp shared his assessment, although they warned that the 5,000 sq. km allocated to the Jewish state – less than the areas of Kent and Surrey (or the American state of Delaware) – would not allow any significant growth. Hence, while rejecting the proposal's specifics, the ZO sought ways to expand the territory a partitioned Jewish state might eventually receive. Recognizing that the presence of Jewish settlements would strengthen Zionist territorial claims, Haganah undertook to ensconce small groups of Jews in parts of Palestine formerly beyond their sights. As part of this programme, fifty-two so-called 'stockade and watchtower' colonies were built between December 1936 and October 1939. The final fourteen were erected in explicit defiance of the 1939 MacDonald White Paper – a further indication that Zionists had now resolved to carry on on their own against both Arab and British opposition, if necessary by force of arms.

Indeed, at the outbreak of the Second World War Jewish Palestine was on the verge of open rebellion against British rule. A primary expression of this rebellion was clandestine immigration. Responding to entreaties from Zionist youth movements in Eastern Europe and spurred by Nazi Germany's expansion into Austria in 1938, Histadrut and the Revisionists established parallel agencies for bringing in immigrants above the British quota. Whereas in 1939 only 11,000 Jews received visas from the mandatory government, 17,000 more entered the country illegally with Zionist assistance, to British and Arab consternation. Other forms of civil disobedience and active resistance to the 1939 White Paper were also planned. However, once war broke out significant parts of the resistance plan were put in abeyance. All but a handful of Zionists believed strongly that their movement's interests, like those of Jews the world over, lay with German defeat, which meant active support for Britain's war effort. Ben Gurion offered a memorable formulation of ZO policy in September 1939: 'We shall fight with Britain against Hitler as if there were no White Paper, and we shall fight the White Paper as if there were no war' (Ben Gurion, 1969: 64).

From war to independence

As had already happened several times in the history of the Zionist movement, it proved easier to coin a slogan than to determine what it should mean in practice.

Most Zionists hoped the war would make it possible not to have to fight the White Paper at all. They saw in that document a mistaken British belief that the goodwill and support of Arabs was potentially more valuable than that of Jews. The war, they were confident, would expose the error: Jews, determined to do all they could to defeat Nazi Germany, would rush worldwide to Britain's aid, while Arabs in Palestine and beyond would equivocate. Indeed, the White Paper had not assuaged Arab anger; in fact, the Palestinian Arab leadership rejected it, because it neither banned Jewish immigration altogether nor explicitly guaranteed a Palestinian state under Arab control. Arabs were also upset that leaders of the 1936–1939 uprising who had fled abroad to avoid capture – most notably al-Husseini – were not given amnesty and allowed to return to the country. In fact, a month after the outbreak of war al-Husseini himself settled in Baghdad, where he agitated openly against Iraq's pro-British government in favour of a pro-German faction. In contrast, when Zionist institutions in Palestine asked in September 1939 for volunteers to serve the British war effort, over 30 per cent of Palestine's Jews – 136,000 people – responded. At the time Zionist leaders expected that Britain would prize their ability to mobilize such a force and reward them, in the short term by withdrawing the White Paper provisions, in the long term by becoming more active patrons of the Zionist programme than they had ever been in the past.

Their expectations were quickly dashed. It was precisely the realistic prospect of Arab–Axis rapprochement that impelled British policymakers to avoid the appearance of giving Zionists even a bit of what they wanted. Thus not only did the British government initially refuse Zionist requests to organize military volunteers from Palestine into distinct Jewish units with a Jewish insignia; it rejected calls to enlarge immigration quotas on humanitarian grounds, prohibited entry of Jews from Nazi-occupied lands even within the quota, fired on a ship containing would-be immigrants lacking visas, took measures to prevent refugees from leaving Europe, enacted the restrictive land ordinance envisioned in the White Paper and actively tried to dismantle Haganah (with which it had happily cooperated during the Arab uprising) by arresting its officers and confiscating its supplies. A bitter Weizmann complained in November 1939 that Britain regarded Palestinian Jews as 'suspects' instead of as 'people whose loyalties and readiness to serve deserve to be encouraged' (in Rose, 1986: 357).

Though all of the British wartime actions galled the Zionists, especially unsettling was the offensive against immigration, since until 1941 Germany was actively extruding Jews from Europe, and Jewish institutions in Palestine could have alleviated the plight of many refugees. More than anything else it was Britain's determination to stop Jews from entering the country that catalysed Zionists' thinking about their movement's purposes and values throughout the war and beyond. 'Fighting the White Paper as if there were no war' clearly implied defying immigration restrictions. Yet not only did defiance endanger the possibility that the Zionist movement might one day gain significant political capital by contributing to Britain's war against the Axis, it both invited additional, potentially crippling, repression and taxed British resources that might otherwise have been used to defeat Hitler. On the other hand, some Zionist leaders asked, how could the movement justify its existence morally if it refused for political reasons to extend its hand to Jews in increasingly dire straits who might escape if Zionists helped them? Although German policy towards Jews did not turn to systematic mass killing until late 1941, and Jews beyond the Nazi orbit did not become aware of the change until a year later, Zionist leaders increasingly understood that the Nazi conquest of Poland in September 1939 had created a situation far more dangerous for the Jewish masses of Eastern Europe than any that had confronted them during the six decades of the Zionist movement's existence. That situation seemed to demand that the movement shift its focus entirely from 'redemption' to 'rescue', even if both the overall war against the Nazis and the future of the Zionist enterprise in Palestine were endangered in the process.

The ZO, the Jewish Agency and their affiliated institutions did not resolve this dilemma: their actions regarding clandestine immigration during the war showed more vacillation than resolve. Nevertheless, the bind in which they found themselves persuaded the large majority of Zionists that the ability to determine who entered Palestine was essential no matter what balance between 'redemption' and 'rescue' they might strike. As a result, from 1940 a 'Jewish state' became the consensus Zionist political aim. In November 1942 the ZO Executive approved a statement (called the Biltmore Programme, after the New York hotel where it had been drafted the previous May) urging 'that the Jewish Agency be vested with control of immigration into Palestine . . . and that Palestine be established as a Jewish Commonwealth' immediately upon Allied victory. 'Commonwealth' envisioned that the Jewish state might become part of a larger federation, but the demand that Zionist institutions alone establish and administer Palestine's immigration policy bespoke an unequivocal Zionist push for territorial sovereignty, including rule over Palestine's Arabs. Biltmore also signalled the end of the Weizmann–Labour preference for gradual development under the leadership of halutsim. By the time it was adopted Zionists of all stripes agreed that Palestine must be prepared to settle millions of European Jews displaced by war.

Only after Biltmore did it become clear that the Nazi Holocaust had made the number of displaced Jews vastly smaller than initially imagined. Ironically, though, it was the very enormity of Jewish losses in Europe that gave Zionists what Ben Gurion called 'a decisive force that will determine the solution of the Palestine question' (in Engel, 1996: 15). Ben Gurion expected that about 650,000 Holocaust survivors would be emotionally unable to rebuild their lives in their former places of residence and would seek to enter Palestine, creating pressure on Britain to lift the White Paper restrictions. If these could be brought to the country, he reasoned, Jews would finally have a majority and could claim state power. As it happened, the general thrust of Ben Gurion's predictions, if not their specific details, was largely borne out. Survivors returning to many East European countries encountered inhospitable, at times violent receptions, inducing some 250,000 to seek refuge in Displaced Persons' camps operated by the United States and Britain in Germany and Austria. These Jewish DPs repeatedly refused repatriation and demanded resettlement, whether west of the emerging Iron Curtain or in

Palestine. The United States preferred Palestine as the primary resettlement destination, if only to deflect pressure to modify its own immigration policies. Accordingly, in summer 1945, US President Harry Truman (1884–1972) called upon Britain to rescind the White Paper and admit 100,000 Holocaust survivors to Palestine immediately.

Britain balked, now convinced that any concessions to Jewish interests would arouse so much Arab anger as to impair vital British interests throughout the entire Middle East. In response Zionists, free from wartime constraints, went on the offensive. Part of their response was military. Having outlasted British efforts to crush it, Haganah, its ranks, arsenals and training levels augmented by Palestinian Jewish soldiers returning from service in the British army, joined with two smaller clandestine military groups with Revisionist ties to form a 'Hebrew Rebellion Movement', which attacked British installations and sabotaged infrastructure. Another part involved resumption of illegal immigration. Between April 1945 and January 1948, 63 ships carrying over 70,000 would-be immigrants tried to land in Palestine without British authorization. Only about 5,000 Jews made it through the British blockade; of those who were caught, some 52,000 were deported to detention camps in Cyprus. The sight of Jewish Holocaust survivors being forcibly turned away from their ancestral homeland and held behind barbed wire under armed guard created a worldwide groundswell of sympathy for the Zionist cause, to which President Truman lent public support.

The damage to its prestige created by the measures to stop illegal immigration, together with the £40 million annual cost of maintaining the mandatory administration, proved too much for

Britain, economically devastated by the war and reduced to the rank of America's junior ally in the emerging confrontation with the Soviet Union. In February 1947 it announced its intention to return the Palestine mandate to the United Nations (successor of the League of Nations, which had entrusted it with the mandate in 1922), leaving the new world organization to determine the country's future. Six months later a UN Special Commission on Palestine (UNSCOP) put forth a new partition scheme: 55 per cent of Palestine west of the Jordan would become a Jewish state and 45 per cent an independent Arab state, with Jerusalem governed by an international regime. Though their leaders had hoped for more expansive borders, the ZO and the Jewish Agency (whose executives had been combined in 1937) greeted the UNSCOP proposal favourably, chiefly because it gave them what they had come since the 1930s to value most of all – the sovereign power to bring Jews into Palestine free of externally-imposed limits. In contrast, Palestine's Arab leaders rejected partition out of hand, in accordance with their longstanding practice of refusing anything less than complete control of the country's government. Britain, still tying its Middle Eastern interests with Arab good will, took their side.

The UN was not moved by British or Arab objections, however. With the rare agreement of the United States and the Soviet Union (which hoped to exploit the future Jewish state as a base from which to expand its own influence in the Middle East), the General Assembly accepted partition on 29 November 1947. On 14 May the following year Britain's last High Commissioner left the country; that afternoon Ben Gurion proclaimed 'the establishment of the Jewish state in Palestine, to be called the State of Israel'.

Recommended reading

Most statements of British Policy are accessible online: the Hope-Simpson Report (http://www.jewishvirtuallibrary.org/jsource/History/Hope_Simpson.html); the Passfield White Paper (http://www.jewishvirtuallibrary.org/jsource/History/passfield.html); the 1931 MacDonald letter (http://www.jewishvirtuallibrary.org/jsource/History/MacdonaldText.html); a summary of the Peel Commission Report (http://www.jewishvirtuallibrary.org/jsource/History/peel1.html); and the 1939 White Paper (http://www.yale.edu/lawweb/avalon/mideast/brwh1939.htm). The Shaw Commission Report is available only in printed form: *Report of the Commission on the Palestine Disturbances of August, 1929*, Cmd. 3530 (London: H M Stationery Office, 1930). Also, the Zionist Biltmore Programme can be found at http://www.mideastweb.org/biltmore_program.htm.

A careful analysis of the effects of Jewish settlement on the Arab peasantry is Kenneth W. Stein, *The Land Question in Palestine, 1917–1939* (Chapel Hill: University of North Carolina Press, 1984). On Britain's strategic difficulties in the Middle East, see Michael J. Cohen and Martin Kolinsky, *Britain and the Middle East in the 1930s* (New York: St. Martin's, 1992). Cohen is also author of a standard work on Britain's Palestine policy during the 1930s and 1940s: *Palestine, Retreat from the Mandate* (New York: Holmes and Meier, 1978). The application of the White Paper policy is ably described in Ronald W. Zweig, *Britain and Palestine during the Second World War* (London: Boydell Press, 1986).

The evolution of Zionist attitudes towards use of armed force in the face of developments in Palestine during the 1930s and 1940s is the subject of Anita Shapira's masterpiece, *Land and*

Power (New York: Oxford University Press, 1992). Yehuda Bauer's *From Diplomacy to Resistance* (Philadelphia: Jewish Publication Society, 1970) is the classic analysis of Palestinian Jewish military and diplomatic activity during the Second World War. The development of Zionist policy during the same period is considered from the perspective of American Jewry in Aaron Berman, *Nazism, the Jews, and American Zionism* (Detroit: Wayne State University Press, 1990). The standard work on wartime Jewish illegal immigration is Dalia Ofer, *Escaping the Holocaust* (New York: Oxford University Press, 1990).

Arieh J. Kochavi, *Post-Holocaust Politics* (Chapel Hill: University of North Carolina Press, 2001) details diplomatic wrangling over the fate of Jewish DPs and British efforts to keep them out of Palestine. An iconic illegal immigration ship serves as the focus for Aviva Halamish's study of the DP role in the postwar Zionist struggle for statehood, *The Exodus Affair* (Syracuse: Syracuse University Press, 1998). The same subject is treated in controversial fashion by Idith Zertal, *From Catastrophe to Power* (Berkeley: University of California Press, 1998).

CHAPTER 6

Movement and state, 1948–1967

ON 15 MAY 1948, the day after he declared Israel's independence, Ben Gurion broadcast his first address as the new state's interim prime minister. 'Yesterday something happened to the Jewish people', he began, displaying uncharacteristic understatement. 'Only the generations to come will be able to assess its full significance' (Ben Gurion, 1969: 107). While he was speaking, Egyptian planes bombed Tel Aviv, dramatically underscoring that Israel's creation was not accomplished peacefully. Ever since the UN General Assembly had voted for partition six months earlier, Palestine had witnessed daily armed battles between Jews and Arabs. Within eight hours of the independence proclamation, five Middle Eastern states – Egypt, Transjordan, Lebanon, Syria and Iraq – declared war, hoping to prevent partition and to impose their own solution on the country. In his diary Ben Gurion summed up the situation laconically: 'At 4:00 pm . . . the state was established. Its fate is in the hands of the security forces' (105).

The security forces did their job. By January 1949 they had not only driven away the last invading soldiers but had pushed into territory beyond the boundaries designated by the UN partition plan. After concluding armistice agreements with four belligerent neighbours, Israel found itself controlling 20 per cent more land than anticipated, including the entire Galilee and Negev Desert, the Tel Aviv–Jerusalem corridor and the western neighbourhoods of Jerusalem itself. The international enclave that had been envisioned for Jerusalem never came into being; instead, the city was divided between Israel and Transjordan (renamed Jordan in April 1949), which also occupied most of the areas the partition plan had designated for the Palestinian Arab state (whose creation Jordan and Egypt effectively aborted). In May 1949 Israel assumed a seat in the United Nations.

When Herzl predicted in 1897 that a 'home for the Jewish people in Palestine secured by public law' would arise within half a century, he had not anticipated how his prediction would materialize. Indeed, little in the actual course of Israel's genesis matched the disparate visions and predictions of Zionism's nineteenth-century intellectual forebears. The Zionism that led proximately to the events of 1948 was rather the product of ongoing recalibration of the point of equilibrium among ideas that were often in tension with one another.

Zionists had long called the framework that united proponents of these various ideas a 'movement' – an apt label for a group constantly changing not only tactics and strategy but the very goals it professed. But now, having achieved its primary stated goal, would the movement continue to move? For three decades the ZO and the Jewish Agency had operated as a quasi-government for Jewish Palestine. Once the task of government passed to the State of Israel, what remained for those organizations to do? Clearly, if the movement was not to vanish altogether, it would need to remake itself once again.

Soldiers, immigrants, and the 'new Jew'

Whether Zionism continued to have any meaning and Zionist institutions any genuine functions following Israel's establishment depended largely on what the state needed from them. As it turned out, those needs have never suggested a single, unambiguous answer. On the contrary, although conditions in Israel have repeatedly generated new sets of problems, both intellectual and practical, the search for whose solution has spurred Zionists to keep their movement in motion by reformulating its principles and ideals, the same conditions have simultaneously created new tensions, making both the movement's values and its proper role in Jewish and Israeli affairs matters of ongoing controversy.

One problem that surfaced immediately upon the state's proclamation was reflected in Ben Gurion's observation that the country's fate depended on the degree to which Palestine's Jews could successfully deploy military force. Diaspora Jews had not habitually cultivated martial virtues, and Zionists, for all their keenness to alter longstanding Jewish behaviour patterns, had initially found other features of diaspora life in more immediate need of repair. Indeed, the 'new Jew' that Zionists expected settlement in Palestine to create was generally depicted during the movement's first half century as a paragon of peaceful living. Smolenskin and Lilienblum, Pinsker and Herzl, Ahad Haam and Weizmann – each had his own notion of what the future

Palestinian Jew would be, but none gave the warrior pride of place. Jabotinsky, who during the 1920s admonished Zionists that only by adopting the most stringent military discipline and the most sophisticated military technology could they create the 'iron wall' behind which they would build the Jewish national home, was at first an exception, his fondness for uniforms and close-order drills regularly mocked in the Weizmann–Labour camp. That camp held up a different ideal – the irenic farmer, armed only with spade and plough, reclaiming a once-fertile land gone to ruin after centuries of neglect by a succession of foreign imperial rulers. To be sure – so ran the dominant pre-state Zionist formulation – farmers occasionally required protection from thieves, and Jews should be able to provide such protection for their own. Accordingly Second Aliyah halutsim organized a professional guard force called *Hashomer* (The Watchman), replaced in 1920 by the part-time volunteers of Haganah. Neither group's activities, though, matched the prestige the Zionist leadership assigned agricultural settlement.

The 1936 Arab revolt catalysed the beginning of a change: for the first time major figures in the labour movement began to depict the ideal 'new Jew' as one with hoe in hand and rifle on the shoulder. The circumstances under which statehood was achieved deepened the process, as did the fact that even after defeating its enemies on the battlefield Israel remained surrounded by states that denied its legitimacy and remained officially at war with it. In consequence, cultivation of military prowess evolved into a paramount Zionist value, with the Israel Defence Forces, organized on 31 May 1948 as successor to Haganah, cast as an emblem of Zionism's noblest traditions and aspirations. In September 1949 Israel enacted universal conscription for male and female Jewish residents, creating a citizen army capable of mobilizing nearly 15 per cent of the country's inhabitants at any time – a force level 14 times that of the United States (though only half that of Switzerland, after whose armed services the Israeli military system was patterned). Ever since, military service has been a formative experience for Israeli Jews (especially men), with a good military record a key to individual success.

Indeed, turning Jews, both men and women, into effective soldiers was soon declared a primary Zionist purpose. Despite the novelty of this declaration, however, most Zionists asserted that the new state's formidable security needs would not deflect their movement from its longstanding goals, however they defined them. On the contrary, Ben Gurion, who became Israel's first defence minister as well as its prime minister, identified the military as an essential instrument not only for maintaining statehood but for achieving classic Labour Zionist socio-economic aims as well. Accordingly he worked to link military service and agricultural settlement. Under his direction the army made farming part of soldiers' training, sending many to found fortified *kibbutzim* and cooperative villages along Israel's 960-km land frontier, in the expectation that they would remain there once their tour of duty ended. Also, decisions about where to place new civilian settlements came to be governed largely by strategic considerations, with preference given to border regions, areas with large Arab concentrations and the country's northern and southern extremes. Soon the military extended its influence into other areas of civilian life. Together with high schools and youth organizations it operated a voluntary Youth Corps, aimed at introducing boys and girls aged 13–17 to skills required of soldiers and involving them in peacetime national service projects like afforestation and roadbuilding. This body's task, Ben Gurion proclaimed, was 'to turn the youth into the main lever for bringing about the moral, cultural, and social change' needed to produce the latest incarnation of the Zionist 'new Jew' (Ben Gurion, 1980: 172).

The military also played a key role in tackling another problem the Zionist movement confronted during the state's first decade – mass immigration. What had impelled Zionists to press for statehood throughout the 1940s and to go to war to achieve it was ultimately the thought that only if they exercised sovereign control of Palestine's borders could they help Jewish refugees and survivors of the Nazi onslaught rebuild their lives in the Jewish national home. When the establishment of the state finally gave them that control, over 140,000 Jews remained in European DP camps, with 50,000 more who had earlier tried to run the British immigration blockade still detained in Cyprus. Thirty years earlier the prospect of many fewer potential immigrants descending upon the country in one fell swoop had moved Zionist leaders to discourage all but those who could build infrastructure from coming. Now such practice appeared contrary to what was universally represented as one of Zionism's basic tasks – the 'ingathering of the exiles' into the historic Jewish homeland. Indeed, the Declaration of Independence promised explicitly that 'the State of Israel will be open to the immigration of Jews from all countries of their dispersion'. Not only was Israel's provisional government determined to offer a permanent home to Jews who had yet to find one after the Holocaust; it actively encouraged Jews from every country to join a new mass *aliyah*.

This new Zionist emphasis on making the State of Israel not only the cultural but the demographic centre of the Jewish people was born largely of the circumstances in which the state came into existence. Israel's new army required manpower: although the nearly 30,000 troops it could deploy in May 1948 matched the size of the force the Arab states and Palestinian Arabs initially committed to battle, intelligence estimates warned that that force might quickly grow five times over. The army counted on immigrants to help make up the difference. As early as March 1948, two months before proclamation of the state, Haganah sent emissaries to DP camps to mobilize Jewish men and women aged 17–35 and begin their military training. Between May and December 1948, nearly 22,000 newcomers, almost all DPs or Cyprus detainees, were conscripted upon arrival in the country. About 400 died in battle.

Draftees accounted for only about a fifth of more than 100,000 Jews who entered Israel during that interval, however. The rest also came overwhelmingly from countries formerly within the Nazi orbit. Speaking more than a dozen languages, one-third without elementary education, most damaged emotionally and many physically by recent trauma, these new arrivals were sometimes callously labelled 'poor human material' by state officials still accustomed to the old Zionist practice of seeking immigrants who matched the haluts ideal. Nevertheless, for all the economic burden they presented, their inability to contribute directly to the war effort and the prejudices they aroused towards the physically feeble, petty bourgeois, 'unproductive', 'old' European Jewish type from whom the Labour Zionist elite recoiled, state policy still viewed their presence as an asset and welcomed them without restriction.

Their value lay first of all in their effect on the country's demographic balance. Demographic issues worried Zionist leaders greatly after the UN partition plan left the Jewish state with an Arab minority of 400,000 – nearly 40 per cent of its population. The 1948 war mitigated those worries only somewhat. Three-quarters of the Arabs in question fled or were chased from areas designated for the Jewish state; several hundred thousand Arab residents of the additional regions Israel added in the course of repelling the invading armies became refugees as well. Nevertheless, 150,000 Arabs remained in Israel following the armistice, and international pressure for repatriating the refugees was considerable. The prospect that Israel would have only the barest Jewish majority thus loomed large in the imagination of the state's leaders.

To be sure, until the late 1930s most Zionists would have been delighted with any majority, no matter how slim; the thought that Jews in Palestine would ever be more numerous than Arabs appeared a distant vision. But in 1937 the Peel Commission had suggested that partition be accompanied by a negotiated 'exchange of populations' similar to the one between Greece and Turkey following their war in 1922, so as to leave both the Jewish state and Arab Palestine with the smallest possible minorities. That suggestion had fired Zionist imaginations; now it was possible to think of a future state as 'Jewish' not only by international recognition of the right of Jews to dominate its government but by the inclinations of virtually all of its inhabitants. Such was how the bulk of the Zionist leadership understood the optimal 'Jewish state' in 1948: non-Jews (especially Arabs) might live in it and enjoy all rights of citizenship, but their numbers should be small enough compared to the

Jewish population that their impact on public life would be minimal.

Israel's leaders were thus not sad at all to see so many Arabs leave its borders during the fighting in 1947–48; in fact, towards the end of the war some military commanders actively worked to push Arabs across the border, with varying degrees of encouragement from different government branches. Still, the 150,000 who remained on Israeli territory seemed to many to constitute an unacceptably high proportion relative to the 650,000 Jews in the country when the state came into being. This perception not only dictated Israel's adamant opposition to the return of Arab refugees, it reinforced the imperative to bring as many new Jewish immigrants into the country as possible, as quickly as possible, no matter how great or small their prospects for becoming the sort of 'new Jews' the state esteemed most.

Israel's efforts to increase its Jewish population succeeded remarkably: within three years the number of Jews in the country more than doubled, and the proportion of Arabs was reduced to around 10 per cent. But success bred difficulties as well. Immigration at such a pace, whose average *monthly* rate of 18,000 equalled the *annual* average under the mandate, would have tested even the healthiest economy, let alone one disrupted by war, boycott and a British freeze of the state's sterling reserves. As a result of mass immigration, moreover, the collective profile of Israel's Jewish community moved even farther away from what the state's leaders would have preferred had demographic pressures not pushed them as they did: after 1948 the percentage of immigrants from Europe declined rapidly, until by 1950 fully 70 per cent of newcomers came from the Middle East and North Africa.

Many Zionist leaders viewed the arrival of so many Jews from those regions – 112,000 in 1949, 120,000 in 1950, 125,000 in 1951, most of them refugees from mob violence or punitive administrative practices introduced in reprisal for the Arab battlefield defeat – as a mixed blessing. The Zionist movement was the creation mainly of Jews from the former Russian and Austro-Hungarian empires, which in 1880 had housed three-quarters of all Jews in the world. The movement's founding fathers had thus assumed that Jews from those places would dominate the Jewish national home. Once the Nazi Holocaust took the lives of nearly two-thirds of European Jewry, however, Zionists began to look to Jews from the Islamic world, who numbered nearly 1.5 million in 1939, to provide the future Jewish state with much of its needed population reservoir. But in significant segments of the movement – especially in Labour circles – dependence upon those Jews aroused considerable anxiety, rooted largely in European stereotypes of the backward 'East', as well as in the realization that few non-European immigrants had been imbued with the pioneering spirit. Ben Gurion expressed this anxiety even as he spoke of the importance of reaching out to Jews from Islamic countries. 'They are farther removed from labour than Polish Jews', he cautioned; 'it will be harder to teach them [labour Zionism] than [to teach Jews] in Poland and Romania . . . because they are more downtrodden and degraded'. Thus, he observed, 'intensive educational work will be required to bring them to a life of labour' (in Tsur, 2001: 239).

In light of the broad nationbuilding tasks with which it was entrusted, it is not surprising that the army served as the chief agency for moulding immigrants from the Middle East and

North Africa into 'new Jews'. As what Ben Gurion called 'the unifying forge of the nation', the army, at the prime minister's instigation, took up such decidedly non-military functions as 'teaching . . . immigrant youth the [Hebrew] language, [the geography of] Israel, the history of the [Jewish] nation, the values of Zionism, and a sense of being a free citizen' (Ben Gurion, 1980: 169). Accordingly, during the 1950s, the military became the state's largest educational institution. As part of their service, soldiers (mostly women) opened schools in immigrant villages, transit camps and settlements distant from major population centres. Conscripts whose educational level was deemed sub-standard were taught reading, writing, arithmetic and civics while in uniform. Ben Gurion regarded the army's involvement in such activities as essential for bringing about 'the rapid fusion of exilic communities' into 'a single historic unit, [sharing] a common will, aspirations, language . . . and creative impulses – in short . . . a nation' (172).

Such dependence upon the military not only for security but for education and immigrant integration did not give generals a dominant role in formulating state policy. On the contrary, Israel established a civilian regime headed by veteran Zionist leaders and supported by the political parties that had been represented in the ZO; the army acceded to their authority with little question. Nevertheless, extending the army's role far beyond strictly military functions signalled a fundamental change for the institutions and customary practices of the Zionist movement. Before the state was created, socializing Jews to the Zionist ethos had been the responsibility of the ZO, the Zionist political parties and a myriad of social and cultural associations affiliated with them. These were voluntary bodies whose members and leaders came from both Palestine and the diaspora. The ZO exercised little central control over how its constituent and affiliated groups went about this task. Instead it was up to each party and association to determine for itself how to define Zionism's assumptions and aspirations for its members and what actions were required in order to be part of the Zionist enterprise. But once socialization became the duty of state agencies – not only the army, but also the public schools and the state radio – the voluntary Zionist organizations, including the ZO itself, lost much of their ability to shape their members' lives. In fact, by preferring state institutions to movement ones as moulders of the 'new Jew', Ben Gurion – who, after supplanting Weizmann as ZO president in 1946 dominated the movement as had no one, even Herzl, before – effectively declared much of the former Zionist apparatus redundant.

Citizenship vs peoplehood

Indeed, Ben Gurion, along with most Israeli leaders, whose Zionism had led them to move to Palestine before Israel's establishment, believed that with the state's creation all who considered themselves Zionists would do the same, effectively liquidating the Zionist movement everywhere else or converting it into a sort of international travel agency for Jews facing the technical and logistical difficulties of relocation. From the movement's earliest days, Zionist thinkers had conceived of Jews throughout the world as members of a single 'nation' and had ascribed to them a uniform political will, represented by the ZO. Therefore, Ben Gurion and his Israeli colleagues reasoned, once the ZO officially proclaimed the Jewish nation's will to territorial sovereignty in Palestine, and once the instrument for exercising that sovereignty – the State of Israel – came into being, Jews everywhere were bound to give the state their undivided loyalty and place themselves under its jurisdiction. They also saw the state's existence and its opening to mass Jewish immigration as a signal that the time had finally come for all Jews, not merely a vanguard of halutsim, to reconstruct their lives in accordance with Zionist socio-economic and cultural ideals. Jews could do so, they insisted, only in Israel; hence for them Zionism could no longer have any meaning for those who did not take up residence in the state. Assuming that Jews who did not immigrate would cut themselves off from the Jewish nation, eventually trading their Jewish identity for that of the nation on whose territory they resided, they tacitly predicted that the state would return the label 'Jew' to its ancient political meaning: in the future a Jew would again be a citizen of the 'Jewish state', no more, no less.

Zionist veterans in Israel also depicted concentrating all Jews in the Jewish state as the only sensible response to the recent Holocaust. Indeed, Israel's Declaration of Independence asserted that the catastrophe 'proved anew the need to solve the problem of the homelessness and lack of independence of the Jewish people by means of the reestablishment of the Jewish State, which would open the gates to all Jews and endow the Jewish people with equality of status among the family of nations'. The state's leaders drew clear lessons from the mass murder of European Jews, which, they noted, was initiated by the government of a country – Germany – where Jews had lived and prospered for centuries, where they had gained civic equality, integrated themselves socially and culturally, and felt entirely at home. If German Jews had not been safe from such a calamity, they warned, no Jew anywhere could ever be truly secure wherever they were a minority, no matter how seemingly unassailable their legal rights and social position. Moreover, they admonished, Jews could never entrust their security as a group to anyone but themselves; such security would be possible only if Jews collectively possessed the means to defend themselves physically – means that in the twentieth century could be marshalled only by a sovereign state. From the dominant post-1948 Israeli perspective, the admonition attributed to Jabotinsky, 'Jews, either you liquidate the diaspora or the diaspora will liquidate you', seemed quite on target: the potentially fatal powerlessness of Jews in dispersion had been rendered self-evident by intervening events.

Israeli Zionists were thus profoundly surprised and disappointed when many of their most eminent diaspora colleagues – including ZO President Nahum Goldmann (1895–1982) and the Jewish Agency's American Section Chair Abba Hillel Silver (1893–1963) – preferred to remain where they were. They were offended even more when Silver and other American Zionist leaders insisted that Israelis had no prescriptive right to determine policy for the entire movement on their own. Indeed, Goldmann even spoke of turning the ZO into an instrument for 'securing for the organized Jewish people [throughout the world] a right to participate in deciding the critical issues facing Israel' (Goldmann, 1970: 431). He, Silver and fellow diaspora Zionists assumed that Jews from western countries would not feel nearly the same impulse to transplant themselves to the Jewish state as East European Holocaust survivors or Jews from Islamic lands. In particular, they noted, the six million Jews of the United States, who now comprised more than half of world Jewry, felt entirely rooted in what they saw as their country, fully part of an American nation, with no reasonable fear for their physical safety. Yet not only did they wish to remain Zionists, they denied that either Israeli Jews or the Israeli government should exert dominant influence over the movement.

These Zionists insisted that Zionism continued to have profound meaning for diaspora Jews as both a cultural programme and an innovative way of expressing a modern Jewish identity. Recalling Ahad Ha'am's vision of Palestine as a 'national cultural centre' for Jews who would 'remain scattered on foreign soils' and the Democratic Fraction's emphasis on directing maximal Zionist resources to instilling a Jewish national culture in Jews no matter where they lived – once highly influential ideas that the events of the previous twenty years had relegated to the periphery of Zionist consciousness – they saw the Zionist movement as an essential agent for propagating a new, global Jewish civilization. According to this conception, the movement would be charged with cultivating not only the tangible space within Israel's borders and the 'new Jews' who populated it but also an intangible Jewish public arena, in which Jews from all corners of the diaspora would explore together the full dimensions of their common cultural patrimony and search for new ways to utilize that legacy for both individual self-fulfilment and the betterment of humanity as a whole. The American Zionist thinker Mordecai Kaplan (1881–1983), among the most vocal exponents of this view, defined the purpose of post-1948 Zionism as enabling Jews 'both in Israel and the diaspora [to develop] such interpersonal and intergroup relations as are likely to help us become more fully human' (Kaplan, 1955: 45). According to Kaplan, the worldwide public arena in which Jews could consider how best to fulfil their human potential could exist only if some Jews constituted a majority in a particular country and 'determine[d] the character of the civilization there' (119). Elsewhere, he noted, Jews could hope at best to 'live in two civilizations' simultaneously (122) – a situation that would compel them to conduct their daily lives in the language of another culture and according to its conceptual categories. In his view, only the Hebrew language would provide a common medium through which Jews could 'develop fully the high purposes and ideas implicit in their Jewish heritage' (133). That ancient tongue, in turn, could be adapted to the demands of modern thought only by those who employed it regularly for ordinary everyday communication. Thus after 1948 many diaspora Zionists expressed their Zionism primarily by employing the Hebrew of contemporary Israel as a second language and by constructing their cultural environment around the literature, music, art, thought and scholarship of Jews in the Jewish state, in order to participate as completely as possible in the ongoing development of Jewish civilization.

This understanding of Zionism harkened back not only to Ahad Ha'am and his early disciples but to a fundamental consequence of defining Jews as a modern 'nation' – one that Smolenskin had noted when he first applied the term to the Jewish group in the 1870s. The idea that Jews should think of themselves as a nation comparable to Poles or Czechs was initially articulated not only in response to late nineteenth-century trends in European politics but also in opposition to the way Jews had long understood their collective identity. Traditionally, Jews supposed that the existence of a distinct Jewish people – *Am Yisra'el* – living among other peoples but not part of them was divinely ordained. According to an ancient Jewish myth, God was said to have singled out – 'chosen' – *Am Yisra'el* from all other groups and commanded them to live according to a special set of laws, much stricter than the laws that bound any other human association. Those laws were quite complex, and Jews had to devote considerable time to learning their intricacies in order to make sure that they fulfilled them properly. In fact, by the late Middle Ages Jewish communities often employed professional scholars – rabbis – to teach the laws to other Jews. Rabbis did not make Jewish law, however; they were merely its authoritative interpreters, their authority based not upon divine investiture but solely upon their own scholarly expertise. Sovereignty – the supreme, unchallengeable right to make and enforce law – was believed to be God's alone.

In contrast, thinking about Jews as a modern nation suggested an altogether different locus of sovereignty – the Jewish people itself. Smolenskin placed sovereignty with the Jewish nation as a whole in an 1875 essay exploring how Jewish law might adapt itself to circumstances in which one or another legal prohibition 'becomes a burden upon the people, keeping them from pursuing their livelihood and their interests' (Smolenskin, 1925: 1/28). Rabbis, he argued, could not be counted upon to help lighten the burden, because they 'have nothing in common with those who work for a living, so they can neither know nor understand the distress that the multiplicity of laws causes'. Therefore, he reasoned, in such circumstances 'the people' themselves could rightfully ignore or modify aspects of the divine law on their own authority. Defining Jews as a 'nation' quickly became a way to justify this position; if 'nations' possessed the inalienable right to establish their own states – an increasingly common assertion in Smolenskin's day – then the authority to make laws must reside in the general will of a nation's own members.

Zionist thinkers in both Palestine and the diaspora found much of use in this understanding of Jewish nationhood, especially because it provided them with a basis for claiming leadership of the Jewish people in the absence of rabbinic sanction. Indeed, they eventually pushed it much farther than Smolenskin had in his day. In the early 1930s Gershom Scholem (1898–1981), one of the most prominent intellectual lights of the newly-opened, Zionist-sponsored Hebrew University in Jerusalem, began to propound a view of Jewishness as a constantly-evolving identity: it had no fixed, God-given essence at all but comprised whatever the collectivity of Jews made of it at any given historical moment. For Scholem, the Zionist project was supposed to create optimal conditions for maximizing the Jewish people's collective creativity. Kaplan expressed much the same idea when he wrote, 'Zionism is contemporary Judaism in action; Judaism in action means that the Jewish people is actively engaged in an effort to adjust itself creatively to the contemporary world' (1955: 26). Thus, he maintained, the Zionist movement must continue to help Jews participate in that effort to the fullest, no matter where they lived: 'Zionism exists for the Jews and not the Jews for Zionism' (21).

For this reason diaspora Zionists who thought about Zionism in this way were not prepared to assign Israeli views on the nature and content of Jewish peoplehood any precedence, no matter how willing they were to take their cultural cues from the Jewish state. On the contrary, they held that because the State of Israel, following longstanding Zionist practice, claimed sovereignty in the name not of its citizens alone but of the Jewish people as a whole, all Jews everywhere had a legitimate voice in state policy. For Goldmann, Silver and like-minded

Zionists, the ZO was to be the instrument through which that voice could be expressed.

That the ZO survived Israeli efforts to circumvent it was, however, due less to the force of diaspora Zionist arguments than to the exigencies of contemporary circumstances. The costs to Israel of maintaining the required level of military mobilization and of settling masses of new immigrants far exceeded not only the state's financial capacity but that of local Jewish capital markets as well. Thus from the outset Israel required significant funds from abroad. Moreover, Israel was born into a world in which small states increasingly depended for their security upon the protection and patronage of one of the two emerging rival superpowers, the Soviet Union and the United States. Although the former had supported Israel's creation, by 1950 the latter seemed clearly the potentially more advantageous patron. However, the US foreign policy establishment was sharply divided over whether assistance to Israel conflicted with the American strategic objective of incorporating the entire Middle East into the anti-Soviet containment belt. Israeli diplomats understood that creating what Abba Eban (1915–2002), ambassador in Washington from 1950 to 1959, called 'a public sympathy that would take Israel out of the diplomatic routine' might well tip the balance in their country's favour (Eban, 1977: 157).

Though diaspora Zionists were often reluctant to take up residence in the Jewish state, they were uniformly keen to aid it as fundraisers and political advocates, and Israel could hardly afford to forgo their assistance. Thus, when in 1951 the Twenty-Third Zionist Congress, the first to convene after the state's establishment, called upon Israel to recognize the ZO as 'the representative of the Jewish people in all matters that relate to organized participation of Jews the world over in the development and upbuilding of the country and the rapid absorption of newcomers' (in Halpern, 1969: 239), the state's leaders took heed. On 24 November 1952 Israel's parliament enacted the 'Zionist Organization-Jewish Agency for Palestine Status Law', merging the two bodies into a single 'authorized agency which will continue to operate in the State of Israel for the development and settlement of the country, the absorption of immigrants from the Diaspora and the coordination of the activities in Israel of Jewish institutions and organizations active in those fields' (238). In effect, the government of Israel assigned the Zionist movement the same task that the British mandatory administration had given it – coordinating and financing the migration and settlement of Jews the world over to the national home – so that state funds need not be diverted for that purpose. On the other hand, by referring to the newly-consolidated ZO as an 'authorized agency' instead of as 'the representative of the Jewish people', Israel tacitly disavowed diaspora Zionists' claims that peoplehood should supersede citizenship in determining who called the shots in the Jewish state. The state granted the ZO a 'special status' much as it might have granted any private company an exclusive concession to develop its mineral resources or operate its ports; it did so because the ZO *wanted* to play a role in Israel's social life and Israel welcomed its contribution, not because it possessed any special standing in the Jewish world that *entitled* it to participate in the state's governance.

Nor was the ZO to be Israel's sole diaspora partner. Israeli officials also cultivated philanthropic and political support among Jews who had never called themselves Zionists at all. Such Jews constituted a potentially greater force than diaspora

Zionists, especially in the United States, where the nearly 600,000 Jews affiliated with a Zionist group accounted for only a minority of Jewish households. Hence, beginning in 1951, Israel began marketing state development bonds directly to investors abroad, using synagogues and Jewish community institutions more than Zionist organizations to locate potential backers. It also sought close connections with the American Jewish Committee (AJC), an organization with a strong upper-class constituency founded in 1906 to 'prevent the infraction of the religious rights of Jews in any part of the world . . . to secure for Jews equality of economic, social and educational opportunity; [and] to alleviate the consequences of persecution' (Marshall, 1957: 30). Until 1947 the group had denied that Jews constituted a nation entitled to political sovereignty and publicly dissented from the Zionist Biltmore Programme. On the other hand, it had long taken a benevolent interest in Jewish settlement in Palestine and expressed 'wholehearted sympathy' for Jews who 'yearn for a home in the Holy Land for the Jewish people' (Waldman, 1953: 202). Louis Marshall, the Committee's longtime president, had been the chief non-Zionist supporter of cooperation with Zionists through the Jewish Agency. Though Marshall's death shortly after the Agency's 1929 founding had enabled Zionists effectively to turn that body into an instrument of their movement, AJC had continued to give financial and moral encouragement to Palestinian Jewry in the same way that it concerned itself with the welfare of Jewish communities throughout the world. In May 1947, while emphasizing anew its rejection of Jewish nationalism, it determined that the needs of both Palestinian Jews and survivors of the Holocaust in Europe demanded support for the UN partition plan, and following

Israel's establishment it pledged to 'aid in the upbuilding of [the state] as a vital spiritual and cultural center and in the development of its capacity to provide a free and dignified life for those who desire to make it their home' (*American Jewish Yearbook*, 1950: 562). That attitude came to define the position known as 'non-Zionism' in the Jewish world, as distinct from the 'anti-Zionism' of increasingly marginal Jewish groups that regarded Israel's establishment as a mistake and urged Jews to offer the state no aid or comfort.

To Israeli officials AJC and other non-Zionist groups in the United States and elsewhere seemed far more congenial political advocates and fundraising partners than the ZO. AJC's insistence that Israel spoke only for its own citizens and not for Jews worldwide may have grated on Zionist ideological sensibilities, but it also meant that its leaders were content to give Israel's government a free hand in a way diaspora Zionists were not. In fact, in early conversations with Israeli representatives, AJC spokesmen intimated that they were prepared to speak out against American Zionists' demands for an active voice in Israel's political affairs. That the Committee's leadership was both affluent and well-connected politically could only add to its appeal, to the point where Zionist ideas could not be permitted to undermine a working accord between AJC and the state. Indeed, in 1950, responding to an AJC concern, Ben Gurion even promised the Committee's president, Jacob Blaustein (1892–1970), founder of the American Oil Company and one of his country's wealthiest citizens, that Israel would no longer call upon American Jews to make their home in the Jewish state. 'The Jews of the United States', Israel's prime minister solemnly declared, 'have only one political attachment, and that is to the

United States of America. They owe no political allegiance to Israel' (*American Jewish Yearbook*, 1952: 564).

Ben Gurion no doubt gritted his teeth as he spoke; indeed, members of his own inner circle criticized him for betraying what they saw as fundamental Zionist principles, and in subsequent years Ben Gurion himself honoured his pledge more in the breach than in the observance. American Zionists, on the other hand, did not object to the statement's content but felt piqued that Ben Gurion had not issued it to them. Indeed, the fact that Ben Gurion preferred to negotiate a significant issue in Israel–diaspora relations with an organization representing Jews for whom the Jewish state provided the focus of neither their political nor their cultural aspirations indicated in the first instance that, even following the Zionist movement's triumph on the international political stage, neither current Israeli nor diaspora conceptions of Zionism would dominate the Jewish world. To Israeli leaders diaspora Zionists appeared unwilling to offer either the immigrant manpower or the unconditional fealty they demanded and unable to match the lobbying potential and financial clout of American non-Zionist bodies. Thus when Ben Gurion explained that his promise to Blaustein stemmed from recognition that 'our success or failure depends . . . on our co-operation with . . . the great Jewish community of the United States', he tacitly acknowledged that pragmatic concerns had rendered moot the ideological fissures dividing Zionists from non-Zionists and from one other.

That both sets of Zionist ideas had become functionally irrelevant was dramatically revealed during the early 1950s, when AJC and another non-Zionist philanthropic organization, the American Jewish Joint Distribution Committee, effectively blocked both the government of Israel and the Jewish Agency from representing the Jewish people as a whole in negotiations with the Federal Republic of Germany over restitution of assets stripped from Jews by the Nazi regime and reparations for injuries inflicted during the Holocaust. The Zionist bodies had initially hoped that Israel would be recognized as the sole heir of all six million Holocaust victims and that monies received would be devoted exclusively to offsetting the costs of settling survivors in the country. However, the non-Zionist organizations proved able to manoeuvre the Jewish Agency, eventually with Israel's assent, into collaborating with them in claiming compensation separately from the Jewish state. Monies received from that claim between 1954 and 1966 were used largely to support rebuilding European Jewish communities instead of 'ingathering the exiles' into the Jewish homeland.

Israeli leaders thus learned that although non-Zionists would not interfere in Israel's domestic affairs, they would also not give the Jewish state a free hand in matters affecting Jews outside the country. They also came quickly to the realization that Israel might not always stand at the centre of their attention. As a result successive Israeli governments have constantly pondered how best to induce non-Zionist Jews in the United States and elsewhere to serve as Israel's champions in their own countries' public arenas. What benefit, they have wondered, could they claim American and other diaspora Jews would derive from putting their political, financial and cultural resources on the line on Israel's behalf?

During the 1950s and early 1960s the principal strategy involved appeal simultaneously to American Jews' predominantly liberal social ideals, widespread identification with foundational

American myths and growing anti-communist sentiments. Israel represented itself to Jews and non-Jews alike as the only democracy in the Middle East, a bulwark against Soviet penetration into the region, a truly just and egalitarian society (epitomized by the institution of the kibbutz), and a country built by immigrants and pioneers 'who set their strength and their spirit against the forces of nature and the allurements of immediate comfort . . . [and] built for their posterity rather than for themselves' (Eban, 1957: 87). This representation surely resonated with American Jewry, as did the image of the fighting Jew who beat back those who would destroy him. Still, before the late 1960s this approach does not appear to have had nearly the mobilizing power for which Israeli leaders hoped. A leading Israeli sociologist noted with alarm in 1957 that over the previous decade 'links between [Israel] and diaspora Jews have become weaker' (Tartakower, 1957: 269), while studies conducted in the United States around the same time suggested that fewer than one-third of American Jews felt it incumbent upon them to offer Israel public support. By the 1960s even the American Jewish Committee had relegated Israel to the lower end of its concerns, after improving interfaith and inter-ethnic relations in the United States and safeguarding the position of Jews behind the Iron Curtain, in Muslim lands and in Latin America. In the middle of the decade worried voices in Israel decried a mounting feeling of alienation between the two primary components of the Jewish world and cast about for ways to overcome it.

A crisis in Israel's relations with neighbouring Arab states, beginning in mid-1967, pointed to a new direction. It also moved a nearly moribund Zionist movement to a new conception of its meaning and mission.

Recommended reading

There is considerable recent writing on the 1948 war, stimulated largely by the opening of hitherto-inaccessible archives. For military and diplomatic aspects and the circumstances of Israel's victory, a good place to begin is David Tal, *War in Palestine, 1948* (London: Routledge, 2004). A more popular treatment is Ahron Bregman, *Israel's Wars* (London: Routledge, 2000); it also contains a chapter on the role of the military in post-1948 Israeli society. The standard work on the Arab refugees produced by the war is Benny Morris, *The Birth of the Palestinian Refugee Problem* (Cambridge: Cambridge University Press, 1987). Morris has added new material and placed his findings in a different light in *The Birth of the Palestinian Refugee Problem Revisited* (Cambridge: Cambridge University Press, 2004). His *Righteous Victims* (New York: Alfred A. Knopf, 1999) offers a readable and authoritative summary of the Zionist–Arab conflict from the 1880s to the end of the twentieth century.

Relations between the Israeli leadership and the American Jewish Committee during Israel's first decade are the subject of Zvi Ganin, *An Uneasy Relationship* (Syracuse: Syracuse University Press, 2005). A glimpse into the politics of the differing positions of Israeli and American Zionists following Israel's establishment can be obtained from Marc Lee Raphael, *Abba Hillel Silver* (New York: Holmes and Meier, 1989). Valuable background to the conflict, stressing the rise of American Zionists to prominence in the Zionist movement during the Second World War, is provided by David H. Shapiro, *From Philanthropy to Activism* (Oxford: Pergamon, 1994). On the Israel–diaspora relations as reflected in reparations negotiations with Germany, see Ronald W. Zweig, *German Reparations and the Jewish World* (London: Frank Cass, 2001).

CHAPTER 7

Normalizers and messianists, 1967–2008

ON 13 MAY 1967 the Soviet Union provided Syria and Egypt with false intelligence that Israel – concerned by a Syrian project to divert the headwaters of the Jordan River that threatened its primary water supply – had massed troops along its northern border in preparation for a surprise attack. Identifying its interests with the Syrian Ba'ath regime, Egypt responded by blockading Israel's Red Sea port of Eilat and placing 100,000 soldiers and 1,000 tanks along the Israeli border. Though Egyptian President Gamal Abd'el Nasser (1918–1970) evidently hoped only to dissuade Israel from its purported plan, bellicose rhetoric made his intentions seem far more ominous. On 25 May Cairo Radio proclaimed that 'the Arab people is firmly resolved to wipe Israel off the face of the earth' (in Tessler, 1994: 393); the following week Ahmed Shukeiri (1908–1980), founding chairman of the Palestine Liberation Organization (PLO), reportedly boasted that in the imminent confrontation 'no Jew will remain alive' (in Shemesh, 2003: 72).

To Israelis, barely a generation removed from the Nazi Holocaust, such threats aroused existential fears. 'Just as Hitler believed that he could not realize his imperial ambitions without annihilating Europe's Jews, so Nasser regards the annihilation of Israel as an integral part of his plan', wrote veteran Mapai activist-turned-critic Eliezer Livneh (1902–1970) (in Segev, 1991: 367). International efforts to broker a peaceful retreat from the barricades were likened to the infamous negotiations at Munich in 1938. Nasser, like Hitler, Israelis believed, could be stopped only by force, and if the international community would not do its duty, only Israel's army would stand in defence of the Jewish people. Accordingly, on 5 June Israel launched a pre-emptive strike against Egypt. Soon thereafter Syria and Jordan joined the fray. In the ensuing war, which lasted but six days, Israel decisively defeated its attackers, wresting control of extensive territories from all three states in the process.

Boundaries fell not only in the Middle East; the wall between Jews in Israel and the diaspora that had been growing over the previous decade and a half collapsed as well. Israel's ambassador to France noted a 'total revolution' among that country's Jews following the Egyptian mobilization: where once the Jewish state was largely peripheral to their identity, now they rushed to aid it with money, supplies and blood. Similarly, a leading American Jewish communal spokesman and public intellectual wrote of 'an abrupt, radical, and possibly permanent change' among Jews in the United States beginning in the third week of May. The change, he opined, ran deep: 'very large numbers of American Jews now feel their Jewish identity more intensely than they have for at least a generation'. Moreover, he observed, whereas in the past American Jews had shied away from behaviour that might be interpreted as expressing 'dual loyalty', they had now come to evince a 'sense of belonging to the worldwide Jewish people, of which Israel is the centre', without worrying 'about what the rest of the world might be thinking of their feelings or of the actions through which they have been expressing these feelings' (Hertzberg, 1979: 210, 218–19). Apparently the prospect that twice within a quarter century masses of their co-religionists might be slaughtered while they themselves went about their daily business in comfort and safety touched a nerve whose existence many had not suspected earlier. When that prospect was obviated by the success of Zionist 'new Jews' in deploying military force, the entire Zionist ethos seemed vindicated.

Some acknowledged that vindication with their feet. Within a single year, from 1968 to 1969, immigration to Israel from North America and South Africa increased sixfold; from Britain it quadrupled, from Argentina it tripled, from France it doubled. Numbers remained small relative to the size of those Jewish communities, to be sure (6,419 from the United States, Canada and Mexico combined), but the trend was striking, and the following year it continued. Immigrants from the western hemisphere and Western Europe, who had never made up more than 20 per cent of newcomers in any year (usually much less), now constituted nearly half of a stream swelled also by the simultaneous extrusion of most of Poland's 30,000 remaining Jews. More strikingly, not only diaspora Zionist but non-Zionist groups adjusted their programmes and budgets to the new reality. The American Jewish Committee moved Israel to the top of its agenda; its highly-regarded monthly journal, *Commentary*, regularly highlighted the country's affairs and what it portrayed as its crucial role in American Jewish life; and the director of its Communal Affairs Department actually praised American Jews who moved there.

Israelis who observed these trends saw in them a clear sign that diaspora Jews, Zionists and non-Zionists alike, were now more receptive than ever before to Israeli understandings of the Zionist imperative. That perception spurred them to re-evaluate once again the Zionist movement's structure and tasks. Such re-evaluations had become a recurring feature of Zionist Congresses since the state's establishment, but hitherto they had given more weight to diaspora conceptions of Zionism than most Israeli Zionist leaders welcomed. In 1951 the Twenty-Third Congress had supplemented the 1897 Basel Programme with a 'Jerusalem Programme', whose language stressed the movement's fundraising and lobbying functions and suggested that immigration to the Jewish state was an individual choice. A similar tendency was evident in the 1960 revision of the ZO constitution: power in the organization (now renamed the World Zionist Organization – WZO) passed from a small Israeli-dominated Executive to individual constituent associations, including Zionist federations in different countries, worldwide Zionist ideological 'unions' and international Jewish fraternal or religious bodies like B'nai Brith and the World Council of Synagogues, whose members need not declare personal allegiance to any Zionist creed. In effect the 1960 constitution transformed the WZO from a membership into an umbrella organization, with every association free to 'determine the conduct of its affairs' without interference from a central authority. During those years Israeli leaders had compromised with diaspora voices out of a sense of weakness and dependence; now they felt emboldened to attempt a reversal of course. In 1968, at the Twenty-Seventh Congress, they engineered a revision of the Jerusalem Programme, defining the 'aims of Zionism' as 'the unity of the Jewish people and the centrality of Israel in Jewish life, the ingathering of the Jewish people in its historic homeland . . . through *aliyah* from all countries, the strengthening of the State of Israel . . . the preservation of the identity of the Jewish people . . . [and] the protection of Jewish rights everywhere'. At the Twenty-Eighth Congress in 1971 they went even further, pushing through a statement on the 'duties of the individual Zionist' that placed personal commitment 'to implement *aliyah* to Israel' at the top of the list. They also reversed the 1952 amalgamation of the ZO and the Jewish Agency, charging the latter with coordinating fundraising among Zionist and non-Zionist bodies and the former with educating diaspora Jews in the newly-redefined Zionist spirit.

It appears, however, that although Israeli leaders accurately gauged their enhanced prestige among Jews the world over, they initially misunderstood its sources. In the event, the growing prominence of Israel in diaspora Jewish consciousness seems to have signified less a general internalization of the dominant Israeli secular Zionist ethos than a newfound appreciation of the Jewish state's role as representative of Jewish spiritual engagement with the Holy Land. The territories that passed to Israeli control following the 1967 war included some of Judaism's most hallowed sites, foremost among them the Western Wall. For nineteen years the occupying Jordanian authorities had denied Jews access to this and other Jewish holy places and vandalized portions of the Jewish cemetery on Jerusalem's Mount of Olives, traditionally the most coveted Jewish burial ground. Many Jews throughout the world, devout and nonbelievers alike, felt in such deprivation a grievous violation of their collective honour and in Israel's decisive annulment of it the most striking testimony of the Jewish state's ability to lift the heads and straighten the backs of Jews everywhere. Jerusalem, which had previously taken a back seat to Tel Aviv ('the first Hebrew city') and the agricultural settlements in Israeli and Zionist attentions (the movement's name notwithstanding), suddenly figured in Israel and the diaspora alike as the locus of the essential Zionist spirit, with the paratroopers who drove the Jordanians from the Old City raised on high as agents for fulfilling the entire Jewish people's deepest millennial longings. Army Chief of Staff Yitzhak Rabin (1922–1995), never noted for oratorical flights, told a rapt audience less than three weeks following the end of hostilities that the victory in Jerusalem had given those soldiers 'the sense of standing at the very heart of Jewish history'; he spoke of 'the revelation of that hour at the Temple Mount' when it was confirmed that the Western Wall was in Jewish hands (in Allon, 1970: 300). Indeed, virtually everywhere Jews' talk of Israel became suffused with a religious idiom strikingly different from the standard, often quite prosaic Zionist rhetoric of productivization, political sovereignty, self-defence and national cultural reconstruction. It was this idiom that inspired much post-1967 immigration; newcomers, especially from North America and Western Europe, gravitated to Jerusalem and other places with strong Jewish historical connections far more than to settlements established under Zionist sponsorship during the first seven decades of the movement's existence. This trend, in turn, challenged fundamental Zionist assumptions even as its bearers cast their lot with the Zionist project.

Zionism, religion and sacred space

Conceiving Zionism as religious activity wasn't new; the weight the conception carried in Zionist and broader Jewish circles was. Although from their movement's outset Zionists had largely defied rabbinic authority, and Jews who adhered to rabbinic tradition regarded Zionist endeavours with hostility, a small minority of devout Jews maintained that some accommodation with Zionism was not only possible but desirable. Such accommodation, these so-called religious Zionists believed, would further both this-worldly and traditional religious ends – especially the ultimate end of hastening the advent of the Messiah. The most prominent early exponent of this view, Rabbi Shmuel Mohilever (1824–1898), was heir to the minority messianic tradition that viewed mass Jewish settlement in Palestine as a precondition for salvation, and he saw in Herzl's ZO an instrument for bringing such settlement about. He also held that Zionist efforts would relieve East European Jews of the material difficulties and threats to their physical safety that many faced during the final decades of the nineteenth century. Therefore, Mohilever argued, 'our attitude towards those [Zionists] among us who do not observe the religious precepts must be . . . as if fire had taken hold of our homes. . . . Under such circumstances, would we not receive anyone gladly . . . who, though irreligious in our eyes, came to rescue us?' (Hertzberg, 1997: 402).

Few accepted Mohilever's argument, but in 1903 the handful that did organized a religious Zionist party called *Mizrahi* (an acronym for Hebrew words meaning 'spiritual centre'). Mizrahi asked religious Jews to help the Zionists create 'a home in Palestine secured by public law' while working simultaneously from within the movement to deflect its secular tendencies. In particular, it sought to place rabbis in Zionist leadership positions and to ensure that the future Jewish home in Palestine would be governed by traditional Jewish religious law.

Through most of the pre-state period Mizrahi accounted for less than 10 per cent of ZO members. It did, however, establish a notable presence in Palestine when the British mandatory administration named one of the country's most prominent religious Zionists, Rabbi Abraham Isaac Kook, chief rabbi of Palestine. The Chief Rabbinate was a British administrative office, not a Jewish spiritual one; Judaism knows no formal rabbinical hierarchy. Nevertheless, Kook's messianic fervour and personal charisma brought him honour and influence throughout the Jewish world. Shortly after migrating to Palestine in 1904 he claimed to have experienced a mystical vision that persuaded him that the country's repopulation by Jews under Zionist auspices meant that the Messiah was actively preparing to come. He thus anointed the secular Zionist movement as the unknowing servant of the divine plan; once they completed their task of settling Jews in every corner of the historic Land of Israel, secular Zionists would return to traditional Judaism, and the Messiah would appear.

Abraham Isaac Kook (1865–1935)

Born to a rabbinical family in a village near Dvinsk, then in the Russian Empire (today Daugavpils, Latvia), Kook attended the famous yeshiva of Volozhin (Valozhyn, Belarus), where he distinguished himself by both the depth of his learning and his intense regimen of study. He was also known for his unfamiliar custom (generally discouraged by traditional religious Jews) of using Hebrew, the 'holy tongue', not only for liturgical purposes but for everyday conversation. The practice bespoke an early affinity for Hibbat Tsiyon, which he confirmed in a series of articles published between 1901 and 1904. In 1904 he migrated to Palestine and became rabbi of the Jewish community of Jaffa.

In 1921 the British mandatory administration renewed the old Ottoman office of chief rabbi. Kook was chosen to lead the Ashkenazi community, consisting of Jews of European origin. Three years later he founded a yeshiva in Jerusalem, Merkaz haRav Kook (The Rabbi Kook Centre), which employed Hebrew instead of Yiddish as the language of instruction and included works of Jewish philosophy and pietistic literature in the curriculum in addition to the traditional legal texts. This academy became the chief institution through which Kook's messianic philosophy was disseminated. His son, Zvi Yehudah Kook, became head of the yeshiva several years after his father's death. Since 1967 Merkaz haRav has provided the intellectual and practical leadership for the settler movement.

Kook's control of the Chief Rabbinate and success in grooming a cadre of ideological successors gave religious Zionists weight in pre-state Palestinian Jewish politics disproportionate to their relatively small numbers. However, the 1948 partition vitiated his messianic ideology at its core: if Jews could not settle the Jordanian and Egyptian-controlled portions of the Land of Israel, redemption could not be at hand. As a result, following the establishment of the state, Kook's spiritual descendants bided their time. But in 1967, when Israel took control of all of the former mandatory Palestine, messianic religious Zionism re-emerged with a vengeance.

Spearheading the resurgence was Kook's son, Zvi Yehudah Kook (1891–1982). Elaborating on the elder Kook's ideas, Rabbi

Zvi Yehudah, as his followers called him, sketched the process by which messianic salvation would be achieved. As masses of Jews, forced from the diaspora by persecution, gathered in the Land of Israel, he declared, they would spread themselves throughout the full length and breadth of the Land, establishing new settlements everywhere. Soon, he predicted, the intimate contact with the Land's sacred soil demanded by such settlement activity would inspire the settlers to return fully to the traditional Jewish way of life; the Messiah would come when that return was completed. Hence, he proclaimed, the State of Israel was 'the pedestal of God's throne in the world' (in Ravitzky, 1996: 127), called into being 'by order of the Sovereign Lord of the Universe so that the clear commandment . . . to "inherit and settle the Land" would be fulfilled' (in Lustick, 1988: 35). Similarly, he reasoned, Israel's military triumph in 1967 was ordained in heaven so that Jews could populate the entire Holy Land.

However, implementing Rabbi Zvi Yehudah's scenario required cooperation from Israel's government, which regulated settlement on most of the country's territory, including the former Jordanian and Egyptian-controlled parts of Palestine (the so-called West Bank and Gaza Strip), inaccessible to Jews for the previous nineteen years. Thus in August 1967 followers of the rabbi opened a lobbying campaign aimed at turning the government into promoters of their cause. Clearly, though, they could not base such a campaign on Rabbi Zvi Yehudah's theology. After all, the government was dominated by veterans of the Labour movement, for whom Israel existed to benefit Jews in the present, not to usher in the world to come. Most of them initially envisioned returning the newly-captured territories to the Arab states from which they had been acquired once those states signed peace agreements recognizing the 1949 armistice lines as Israel's permanent, legitimate borders. Accordingly, though not opposed in principle to Jewish settlement in the territories, they were inclined sharply to limit its numerical and geographical scope, in order to avoid complicating future diplomatic negotiations. Rabbi Zvi Yehuda's grand messianic visions were hardly likely to dissuade them from this course.

As a result, the rabbi's disciples rooted their appeal in the powerful emotions and religiously-charged rhetoric that had swept Jews the world over – Israel's leaders included – following victory. Those emotions had already moved a group of prominent Israeli artists, intellectuals and elder statesmen from both Labour and Revisionist backgrounds to form a 'Movement for the Whole Land of Israel', which proclaimed that 'now that the entire Land . . . is in the Jewish people's hands . . . we are commanded to preserve it' in the name of the Jewish people as a whole. 'No government', this movement insisted, may relinquish control over any part of the Jewish territorial patrimony, 'which represents the inherent and inalienable right of our people from the beginning of its history' (43). Rabbi Tsvi Yehudah's votaries played even more strongly on the specific historical associations of newly-captured sites like Hebron, Bethel and Shiloh – places fraught with biblical resonance, with which Jews throughout the world could now reconnect after two decades (some would say two millennia) of enforced separation. How, they asked, could the government of a Jewish state legitimately prevent Jews from returning to the bedrock of their existence, to the precise locations where, according to the Declaration of Independence, 'their spiritual, religious, and national identity was formed'? Indeed, they portrayed themselves, not the Labour Zionist establishment, as the rightful heirs of the halutsim; they were now the self-sacrificing vanguard driving radical change for the Jewish people as a whole. A Labour government that opposed them, they suggested, had lost touch with its own heritage and forfeited the right to lead the Zionist movement.

The comparison glossed over obvious discontinuities with the Labour legacy. For one, the would-be settlers in the West Bank and Gaza Strip spurned Labour Zionism's social ideals. In particular, with few exceptions, they did not propose adding to the stock of kibbutzim and cooperative settlements to which the labour movement had long awarded pride of place. Instead, they envisioned a landscape of towns and smaller 'community villages' whose residents sustained themselves through individually-owned local enterprises or by commuting to jobs in the country's main cities. The classic Labour Zionist aim of transforming the Jewish people's economic structure figured little in their minds. Indeed, where socialists like Ben Gurion had understood Zionism as a vehicle for bringing Jews to the land, in the mundane sense of helping them both migrate to Palestine and transform themselves into workers earning their livelihood from the soil, Rabbi Zvi Yehuda's followers appear to have valued it more as an instrument for bringing land to the Jews, in the cosmic sense of restoring ownership of sacred ground without which they could not fulfil their collective destiny. Such elisions notwithstanding, however, the claim that governing and settling all parts of the historic Land of Israel represented the culmination of the Zionist dream proved impossible for Israel's government to resist. Though they tried to regulate settlement in accordance with military and diplomatic needs, Israeli officials ultimately could not say no to messianists seeking first to re-establish Jewish communities abandoned under Arab pressure before or during the 1948 war, then to move masses of Jews into the biblical territories of Judah and Israel.

The claim also demonstrated enormous political mobilizing power – power that grew markedly after a coordinated Egyptian-Syrian attack in October 1973 caught Israel's military and political leaders unprepared. Israel repulsed the threat, but at great cost, and not before the invading armies pushed it to the brink of capitulation. The strategic and intelligence failures that contributed to initial Arab successes eroded public confidence in the Labour Zionist elite that had governed the state since its founding, paving the way in 1977 for *Likud*, a party claiming the mantle of Jabotinsky's Revisionists, to be voted into office. Followers of Rabbi Zvi Yehudah played a major role in this shift. In 1974 they had organized an extraparliamentary pressure group, *Gush Emunim* (Faith Bloc), which, borrowing a page from the Labour-led struggle against the British in the mandate's final days, established settlements without government permission, daring the authorities to remove them. By inviting confrontation, Gush Emunim forced the government, like immigrants running the British blockade three decades before, either to deny Jews the right to reside in the cradle of their history or to relinquish control over settlement policy. If they did the former, the authorities would appear to betray what the religious inflection of post-1967 public parlance had suggested was the essence of the Zionist ethos; if the latter, they would seem indecisive and inept.

Likud and the settlers became fast allies; after all, Jabotinsky and his political heirs had opposed not only the partition proposals of 1948 and 1937 but the 1922 separation of Transjordan from the original Palestine mandate, and the Likud platform proclaimed mass Jewish settlement in the West Bank and Gaza Strip as the surest way permanently to undo what it called the dismemberment of the Jewish homeland. Likud's leaders made Gush Emunim a primary agent of its settlement projects, much as the ZO had elevated the halutsim of the Second Aliyah. Likud's victory thus ensured the messianists serious political clout, the accord between the two effectively replacing the old bourgeois-socialist coalition that had dominated Zionist and Israeli politics for seven decades.

It also spurred yet another reformulation of Zionist ideas, pushing the movement once again in a new direction.

'The sheet anchor of the Jewish people'

From inception, Zionist thinkers and activists of most varieties imagined that success for the Zionist project would 'normalize' relations between Jews and all other human groups. Lilienblum, Pinsker, Herzl, Borochov, Jabotinsky, Ben Gurion – all believed that the antipathy and persecution they saw as constant features of diaspora Jewish history stemmed at bottom from the Jewish people's lack of territorial sovereignty – a condition they regarded as 'abnormal' in a world where nations were expected to constitute states 'of their own'. That belief suggested that once the abnormal condition was corrected, antipathy and persecution would disappear along with it: Jews would no longer be feared as a disembodied spirit, castigated as spongers off others' labour, held in contempt for weakness or abused as eternal foreigners ever at their hosts' mercy. Statehood, they asserted, would and should make Jews 'like all the nations', distinguished from others only by the same sort of cultural markers that separated Germans from Spaniards or Persians from Turks.

Both Likud and Gush Emunim dissented strongly from that view. The former's leader, Menachem Begin (1913–1992), in a sharp departure from Jabotinsky's teachings clearly reflecting the impact of the Holocaust, maintained that Jews were uniquely destined for eternal obloquy and attack. The Jewish state, he taught, could not end that condition; it could only give Jews the weapons they needed to ward off its effects. In his view, Jews were fated to remain, in a biblical phrase he quoted often, 'a people that dwells alone', the State of Israel an outcast among the international community. Gush Emunim ascribed this condition to divine choice and invested it with theological meaning. Its theoreticians took Jews' ability to establish their state and increase its territory against its neighbours' armed might as proof that God was ever on Israel's side and postulated that such divine favour invariably aroused all others' enmity. Thus neither Likud nor Gush Emunim showed much concern that their enthusiasm for populating the post-1967 territories with large numbers of Jews encountered sharp criticism in international fora. Opposition to settlement, they believed, was merely an expression of the fundamental antagonism between 'Israel and the nations' inscribed in the universe's primordial structure; hence attempts to appease it by altering policy could only embolden Israel's enemies and undermine.the state's capacity to defend itself against them.

As it happened, events in the mid-1970s impelled growing numbers of Jews in Israel and abroad to dismiss normalization as utopian fantasy. The 1973 war threatened to scuttle the prospect of reducing Cold War tensions that the recent movement towards détente had aroused. Many governments blamed Israel for the threat, arguing – wishfully, in the Israeli government's eyes – that a prompt return of territories captured in 1967 would have eliminated the provocation for the Egyptian invasion. Concomitant pressure from oil-producing Arab countries induced dozens of Israel's former Third World allies not only to sever diplomatic ties but to denounce the Jewish state as a threat to world peace and security and a purveyor of evil throughout the planet. Israel's isolation reached especially alarming proportions in 1975 when the UN General Assembly, which had endorsed the state's creation less than three decades before, adopted a resolution declaring that 'Zionism is a form of racism and race discrimination'. Jews throughout the world interpreted these developments not only as egregiously unfair condemnation in light of other nationalist movements' often far more heinous and treacherous behaviour but as a sign that Israel, far from eliminating the verbal, political and physical abuse frequently visited upon individual Jews in the past, had become its primary target. If Jewish existence had been 'abnormal' before Israel's creation, it seemed no more 'normal' now.

Yet even as this situation undermined one classic Zionist assumption, it also reaffirmed, for diaspora Jews in particular, the essential role the Jewish state had come to play in their lives. Jews throughout the world understood international castigation of Zionism as directed against them, wherever they lived: in one commentator's words, 'as long as Israel was attacked by name, as a geopolitical territory, Jewish citizens of other lands remained technically dissociated from the target, but the cynical attack on Zionism, drawing no distinction between the politics of the state and its existence, put all Jews on the firing line' (Wisse, 1978: 48).

That observation suggested in turn that the murderous ill-will towards the Jewish people that had generated the Nazi Holocaust was not vanquished together with the Third Reich. To be sure, few western Jews sensed immediate danger of physical annihilation, but the possibility that hostile forces might one day again threaten significant parts of the Jewish world was one for which Jewish leaders increasingly felt need to prepare. Keeping Israel strong militarily and diplomatically seemed to many the best preparation: as long as it remained sufficiently robust, the Jewish state could shelter Jews fleeing aggressive antagonism, and its armed forces could defend them should their lives become imperilled. Not that Jews from western countries felt any greater impulse to congregate there; western Jewish immigration after the early 1970s fell well below its post-1967 peaks. For them Israel figured as a refuge of last resort, nothing more. As an erstwhile American Jewish communist who warmed to Zionism during the 1970s put it, 'After the Holocaust [Israel] is the sheet anchor of the Jewish people' ('American Jews', 1988: 51).

Those who took this position generally measured Israel's 'strength' by its ability to withstand both military assaults and diplomatic pressure to relinquish territory acquired in 1967 before the Arab states made peace. Marshalling resources to maximize US military aid to Israel, minimize aid to its adversaries and deflect foreign initiatives for territorial compromise was thus increasingly defined as the central mission not only of diaspora Zionists but of the far greater number of Jews who identified themselves as 'pro-Israel'. Such activity differed markedly in tone and substance from the ways in which diaspora Jews had assisted Israel during its first two decades. Where earlier the balance between philanthropic and political support fell well towards the former, now politics gained mounting communal attention. Moreover, Jewish leaders explained their support less as an act of generosity towards others in need than as one of collective Jewish self-interest. 'We Are One!' became an American Jewish rallying cry, expressing a profoundly-felt conviction that 'Jews and Israelis shared a common destiny as Zionists – not only for better but, as might also be the case, for worse' (Wisse, 1978: 48).

This newfound sense of belonging to a single, worldwide community of fate impelled many Jews to ponder the source of their ostensibly unique condition. Such curiosity led to a widely-noted upsurge of interest in Jewish history, literature and religion. The religious inflection of post-1967 discussions of Israel appears to have guided much of this quest. *Commentary* editor Norman Podhoretz (1930–), a non-observant Jew and former leftist who emerged in the 1970s as both analyst and exponent of what he termed 'the conversion of America's Jews to Zionism', called the 'reassertion of the will to life' he identified in the revival of Jewish study 'a religious act . . . something not easily comprehended by ordinary categories of contemporary understanding, something touched by the miraculous' (Podhoretz, 1983: 38–9). Thus, ironically, post-1973 anxieties actually intensified the broad religious enthusiasm that the feelings of strength engendered by the 1967 victory first kindled.

That development, in turn, helped diaspora Jews fall in seamlessly behind the leadership of Begin and Gush Emunim. Begin, eager to solidify his alliance with the messianists, readily explained his government's contention that the West Bank (or, as he insisted, 'Judea and Samaria') was an integral part of the Jewish state whose future was not subject to negotiation in language that dovetailed neatly with the world views of both Rabbi Zvi Yehuda's devotees and 'pro-Israel' Jews everywhere. The territories, he consistently asserted, were to be retained not only for the strategic advantages they might provide but even more because they were the sacred preserve of the Jewish people, the fount of its miraculous existence and the embodiment of its ontological right to dispose of the entire Land of Israel for its own purposes. Precisely because that claim was couched in particularistic Jewish terms unfamiliar in 'normal' international diplomatic discourse, many Jews took his government's effort to keep the territories off the negotiating table as a supreme test of Israel's power: if Begin could make it stick, Israel must be sufficiently strong to guarantee that a second Holocaust was not in the offing. Such reasoning also reinforced Gush Emunim's castigation of 'normalization' as a strategy of weakness and embrace of abnormality as a source of strength.

Hence by the late 1970s few continued to count normalization among Zionism's fundamental goals. However, by discrediting that objective, those who rejected it laid the groundwork for an internal Jewish culture war that by the end of the twentieth century led growing numbers of Israeli Jews to wonder whether Zionism according to any conception or historical example remained relevant to their lives at all.

Judaism and the Jewish state

The exordium for that culture war was the very definition of Israel as a 'Jewish state'. Most Zionists understood the notion as a corollary of normalization: just as Poland was a 'Polish state' by virtue of the fact that the bulk of its citizens and governors belonged to the Polish nation, spoke the Polish language and took part in the ongoing development of Polish national culture, so would Israel be a 'Jewish state'. On the other hand, religious Zionists argued consistently that Poland (or any other state) could not serve as an example, because Jews were a people without parallel among the nations of the earth: whereas other nations were free to develop their culture according to their own lights, the fundamental features of the Jews' culture were prescribed by God. Hence, they argued, the adjective 'Jewish' could legitimately be applied only to institutions whose acts were sanctioned by divinely-ordained Jewish law and by rabbis ordained to interpret it. It followed that a 'Jewish state' could not simply be one in which the government was composed of Jews; in a 'Jewish state' the government was required to uphold Jewish religious norms and inculcate them actively in society.

Surprisingly, perhaps, this fundamental ideological difference had little practical consequence during the state's first quarter century. As a small minority among Zionists, Mizrahi supporters were unable to impose their view upon the movement, nor did they wish to alienate the secular majority, whose assistance they required to implement their messianic scenario, by insisting upon it too vocally. Nevertheless, their conception was not without influence in the movement as a whole. The Zionist movement claimed to speak for the *entire* Jewish nation, not only that segment that accepted its conception of the source of national authority. Moreover, Zionists consistently represented themselves as the bearers of authentic Jewish nationhood, unlike Jews who sought integration into the societies and cultures of citizen-based states, whom they denounced as 'assimilationists' – wilful effacers of their heritage. Zionists found it difficult to deny, however, that many of the distinct cultural characteristics that they claimed entitled Jews to inclusion among the ranks of nations stemmed from traditional religious law and practice. Rabbis could attest to their authenticity and fidelity to the Jewish people's historic legacy in a way that no others could. For that reason Zionist leaders since Herzl thought it wise to obtain maximum rabbinic approval, as long as doing so did not compromise the basic principle of popular (as opposed to divine) sovereignty. The fact that such approval was so rare made the support of the relatively few rabbis who became Zionists all the more valuable. Hence the movement consented to conduct its public affairs and those of Palestine's Jewish community in sufficient conformity with Jewish religious law to allow religious Jews to participate fully in its activities: Zionist offices (and Jewish-owned businesses in Palestine) would close on the Jewish sabbath and holidays (when labour was forbidden), and the movement would observe Jewish dietary laws at all official functions. After the state's establishment this agreement continued, as did the longstanding Ottoman and British mandatory practice of considering marriage and divorce religious matters to be governed exclusively by religious law. State support was also given to a system of Jewish religious schools separate from the public schools attended by the large majority of the country's citizens.

This arrangement was motivated less by political necessity than by the deeply-held conviction of secular and religious Zionists alike that their respective goals were best served by cooperation. Maintaining that cooperation despite irreconcilable disagreement over the core meaning of the state's identity required that potentially divisive issues be resolved quietly through pragmatic compromise, not openly through debate in the political arena, which might highlight division. Mutual willingness to handle disputes in this way underlay a decision by Israel's leaders not to formulate a written constitution, which would require codifying one or another conception of Judaism's role in the Jewish state. That willingness evaporated, however, once the post-1977 Likud government appointed Gush Emunim to spearhead its settlement programme. Gush Emunim operated in the spirit of confrontation, not conciliation – a spirit born of the conviction that the time for realizing their messianic plans had finally arrived. Its rise to political influence in spite (and perhaps because) of its aggressive posture emboldened Israel's religious Jews – both heirs of Mizrahi and the so-called ultra-orthodox (spiritual descendants of pre-Zionist Palestinian Jewry who rejected Zionism altogether on the grounds that Jewish political control of the Holy Land should be a result, not a catalyst, of the Messiah's arrival) – to press for implementation of their concept of a 'Jewish state' (or, as the ultraorthodox preferred, a 'Jewish society'). The increasingly religious tone of public discourse in the Jewish world and Begin's enthusiastic embrace of it boosted their assertiveness even further. Thus, after joining Begin's coalition, both the National Religious Party (NRP – successor to Mizrahi) and the ultraorthodox party Agudat Yisrael raised demands for more stringent state enforcement of religiously-derived behavioural norms: the longstanding ban on bus and rail transport on the sabbath should include Israel's national airline and private automobiles in neighbourhoods with religious majorities; exemptions from military service for religious women and rabbinical students should be extended; cultivation and sale of (religiously-enjoined) pork by Jews should be forbidden; and state law should incorporate principles of rabbinic jurisprudence. Some of their demands were enacted. Moreover, state financial support for Jewish religious institutions and schools increased notably, as did curricular emphasis on study of Jewish religious texts in secular public schools – an initiative of newly-appointed Education Minister Zevulon Hammer (1936–1998), one of the founders of Gush Emunim.

These developments raised intense opposition among the secular majority, which complained of 'religious coercion'. Secularists were especially galled by the religious parties' attempt to amend one of Israel's cornerstone laws, the 1950 Law of Return, which (together with the 1952 Nationality Law) offered an immigrant visa and immediate citizenship to any Jew coming to settle in the country. The law did not define who qualified as a Jew under its terms, however, so it fell to Israel's Supreme Court, in accordance with majority Zionist conceptions of Jewishness, to mandate a social criterion: the general sense of the Jewish community should determine who is a Jew, not religious law. Fearing the court's determination might impair religious-secular cooperation, Israel's parliament amended the law in 1970, providing on one hand that 'for the purposes of this law, "Jew" means a person . . . born of a Jewish mother or . . . converted to Judaism and who is not a member of another religion' and on the other that non-Jewish spouses, children and grandchildren of Jews according to this definition were entitled to the same consideration as Jews. The amendment was a compromise; its definition was religiously rigorous, but it also reflected a broad consensus among Israeli Jews that their diaspora co-religionists who had married non-Jews should also be enabled to join them in the Jewish state without forsaking their family ties. Yet though initially acceptable to religious Zionists, the compromise rankled the ultraorthodox, who warned that, by not specifying a specific procedure for conversion to Judaism, it potentially legitimated conversions performed under the auspices of certain diaspora denominations whose relatively permissive interpretation of Jewish law rendered their practices unacceptable according to prevailing Israeli standards. Accordingly, when a thin electoral victory in 1981 left Likud dependent upon ultraorthodox support to remain in power, Agudat Yisrael demanded further amendment of the Law of Return as its price for cooperation. A more aggressive NRP joined the demand, and Begin acquiesced.

The suggested amendment – that the Israeli rabbinate set procedures for diaspora conversions – prompted renewed debate throughout the Jewish world over Israel's proper role in it. Unlike earlier rounds, however, which centred largely on institutional relations, the one that began in the 1980s cut to the heart of Israel's self-definition. Indeed, several aspects of the controversy over the Law of Return deeply troubled the nonreligious Israeli Jewish majority. To begin with, the amendment effectively denied the Jews themselves any voice in determining whom to admit to their ranks; the Jewish people's boundaries were to be set instead by one small segment, claiming divine authorization to act without majority support. That the government could be pressured into abrogating the principle of popular sovereignty upon which the Zionist movement had rested from its inception aroused fears that the movement might not long remain master in its own home – a fear reinforced by religious Zionists' evident readiness to follow the non-Zionist ultraorthodox lead, subordinating their Zionist loyalties to religious ones.

To be sure, over the next quarter century the amendment was raised and defeated repeatedly, but the circumstances of defeat pointed to new difficulties. Organizations in the United States representing the denominations whose conversion procedures were questioned threatened to curtail financial and political support for Israel if the amendment were adopted, and a break with these powerful segments of American Jewry was something Israel could ill afford. Likud, which held or shared power for all but six years between 1977 and 2006, was especially keen on retaining American Jewish confidence, since its settlement practices generally did not chime with the wishes of successive US administrations, and it often needed American Jews to speak on its behalf. For their part, mainstream American Jewish organizations, caught up in the post-1973 equation of settlement with security, were generally inclined to do so, but the conversion issue suggested limits to solidarity. Thus American Jews' readiness and ability to force Israel's hand on that matter demonstrated that even their ostensible mass conversion to Zionism, as they understood it, would not dissuade them from pushing the Israeli government in directions that conformed with diaspora sensibilities; Israel may have been their sheet anchor, but it hardly provided their Jewish compass. Indeed, it could have been but cold comfort for Israeli secularists that the religious offensive was rebuffed only with the assistance of Jews who had no intention of claiming the benefits of the Law of Return themselves. Moreover, American leaders of the challenged denominations did not oppose the amendment because it ran counter to the Zionist assertion of the Jewish people's primacy over the Jewish religion: they insisted merely that their movements' rabbis share the religious authority over which NRP and the ultraorthodox demanded exclusive control. The Israeli and diaspora Jewish majorities were, it seemed, farther apart than ever in their understandings of what Zionism implied.

The religious–secular and the Israel–diaspora fissures continued to widen over the quarter century after the conversion controversy first broke. Divisions also appeared within the camps themselves following Israel's 1982 invasion of Lebanon, as some Jews in Israel and abroad began to question longstanding Zionist ideas about proper use of military force. Organized Palestinian Arab violence in opposition to the ongoing Israeli presence in the West Bank and Gaza Strip, beginning in 1987 (the so-called *intifada*, from an Arabic word for 'shaking off'), further sharpened polarizations along multiple axes. As the 1936 Arab revolt had done to Britain, the Palestinian uprising forced Israel to expend significant military resources to control it, leading planners and, gradually, significant segments of Israel's electorate to doubt the strategic value of continued occupation. In 1992 a small electoral majority, believing that the adamant refusal of Begin and his successor, Yitzhak Shamir (1915–), to consider any alternative for the territories acquired in 1967 besides massive Jewish settlement under permanent Israeli administration no longer enhanced Israeli Jews' personal security, returned the Labour Party (Mapai's successor) to power, largely on the perception of its leader, Yitzhak Rabin (the same former army chief who had termed the capture of Jerusalem's Old City a moment of 'revelation'), as a pragmatist who could reverse fifteen years of ideologically-driven settlement policies and seek a negotiated end to the Israeli–Palestinian confrontation. The following year Rabin's government appeared to confirm that perception by signing a 'Declaration of Principles on Interim Self-Government Arrangements' for Palestinian Arabs in the West Bank and Gaza Strip (the so-called Oslo Accords). The declaration, endorsed simultaneously by the PLO, which formally recognized 'the right of the State of Israel to exist in peace and security' and committed itself to 'a peaceful resolution of the conflict between the two sides', pledged Israel to remove its military forces in the territories from Arab population centres and transfer administrative responsibilities to an elected Palestinian Authority as prelude to a 'comprehensive peace . . . and historic reconciliation'. It was widely assumed that such reconciliation would be based upon establishment of the Palestinian Arab state envisioned in the 1947 UN partition resolution but aborted as a result of the 1948 war, in borders roughly following the 1949 armistice line.

The secular Likud opposed the Oslo Accords as unwise; religious Zionists castigated them as a betrayal of Jewish first principles. Two former chief rabbis declared that Jewish law categorically forbade handing any part of the Land of Israel over to non-Jewish rule and instructed soldiers to disobey orders to withdraw or evacuate settlements, proclaiming religious injunctions superior to state law. Some religious authorities termed Rabin a *rodef* (pursuer), one whom Jewish law justifies killing in order to prevent mortal danger to others. In 1995 a religious Zionist student, acting on this view, assassinated the prime minister. Though no evidence was adduced that the assassin acted with explicit rabbinic sanction, the rabbinic denigration of state authority that tacitly underwrote his deed prompted serious ruminations among secular proponents of settlement and territorial retention about whether continued alliance with organized religious Zionism was advisable. Indeed, since that watershed event many in Israel's secular right wing have retreated steadily from the religious rhetoric that Likud wielded so effectively in the past, couching their position mainly in the mundane language of security and stressing their unshakable commitment to democratic rule. Even more striking, many on the secular right have abandoned absolute opposition to relinquishing territory should security considerations so warrant.

Less transformation has been obvious in the speech or behaviour of mainstream American 'pro-Israel' organizations. Though many have accepted that some measure of territorial compromise might be warranted if it would bring Israel genuine peace and full acceptance by its neighbours, they have often argued simultaneously that Israeli leaders have ceased to be properly mindful of the spiritual needs of the Jewish people as a whole. Fears that Israel was ignoring those needs exploded in 2000, when Israeli negotiators appeared ready to relinquish parts of the Old City of Jerusalem, including the Temple Mount (though not the Western Wall), to Palestinian Arab control in a final resolution of the conflict between them. Leaders of thirty-two major American Jewish organizations, including both supporters and challengers of the Israeli rabbinate's monopoly on conversions, responded with full-page advertisements in American and Israeli newspapers proclaiming that 'Israel must not relinquish the Temple Mount, the Jewish people's holiest site'. They insisted that the Israeli government was not entitled to dispose of sacred Jewish territory on its own, without consulting Jews worldwide. 'In the future', warned one leader, 'we shall . . . have to answer to our children and grandchildren when they ask why we did not do more to protect their heritage and the Temple Mount' (Sheleg, 2001: 3). Israeli diplomats noted similar sentiments among Jews in Britain, France, Latin America and Russia.

The complication of Israel–diaspora relations and the intensification of multifaceted divisions within the Jewish world since the 1980s have beset the Zionist movement with a challenge for which its past offers no ready guide, and doubts have been raised whether its historic stock of ideas can meet it. In particular, the notion that Israel, as a Jewish state, ought to expend precious material, diplomatic and human resources to enhance the spiritual experience of diaspora Jews (and a relatively small proportion of its own Jewish population), even if doing so extracts a heavy strategic and human burden from its residents, has moved part of the country's secular cultural elite to question whether fundamental Zionist assumptions about the purpose of a Jewish state and the values upon which Israel was founded remain valid. So-called post-Zionists have posited a contradiction between Israel's self-definition as a state whose greatest purpose is to serve the needs of Jews throughout the world and fulfilment of basic responsibilities towards its own citizens. In particular, noting that Israeli leaders have long abandoned the core Zionist demand that all Jews settle in the state, they ask whether Israel would not be better off disconnecting from the diaspora altogether, redefining itself not as the state of the Jewish people worldwide but as 'a state of all its citizens', Jewish and non-Jewish alike. They question whether the very concept of a nation-based state is compatible with democracy, a value they argue must trump any particularistic Jewish interest. In order to become a truly democratic society, they argue, Israelis must cultivate a collective identity independent of Jewishness. Hence they have called upon Israel to alter the basic symbols of its sovereignty – its flag, emblem and national anthem – by removing their specifically Jewish references.

Such ideas have attracted much notice in Israel and beyond, but at the end of the twenty-first century's first decade they have yet to demonstrate much practical effect. Instead, the large majority of Jews, in Israel and the diaspora alike, continue to affirm that Israel must be both a Jewish and a democratic state, and the latest revision of the Jerusalem Programme, in 2004, commits the Zionist movement to find a proper synthesis between the two. To be sure, the movement remains sharply divided over what the terms actually mean, what the synthesis between them should entail and how it should be effected. But disagreement on fundamentals has been a constant feature of Zionist history, and there is no reason to expect that it will be any less so in the future.

Recommended reading

The 1960 ZO Constitution can be found, along with descriptions of other Zionist institutions, at http://www.aldeilis.net/english/index.php?option=com_content&task=view&id=1074&Itemid=1. The text of Resolution 3379 of the UN General Assembly, equating Zionism with racism, is posted at http://www.jewishvirtuallibrary.org/jsource/UN/unga3379.html. For the Law of Return, see http://www.mfa.gov.il/MFA/MFAArchive/1950_1959/Law%20of%20Return%205710-1950.

A detailed, blow-by-blow account of the 1967 war is Michael B. Oren, *Six Days of War* (New York: Oxford University Press, 2002). The war's influence on understandings of Zionism in Israel and the diaspora is a central subject of Yosef Gorny, *The*

State of Israel in Jewish Public Thought (New York: New York University Press, 1994), a work that treats the intellectual history of Israel–diaspora relations during the state's first forty years. Attitudes of American Jews towards developments in the Israel–Palestinian conflict since the 1990s are treated in Ofira Seliktar, *Divided We Stand: American Jews, Israel, and the Peace Process* (Westport: Praeger, 2002).

Aviezer Ravitzky, *Messianism, Zionism, and Jewish Religious Radicalism* (Chicago: University of Chicago Press, 1996) offers a sophisticated exposition of both religious Zionist and ultra-orthodox thought in relation to the idea of a Jewish state. Ian S. Lustick, *For the Land and the Lord* (New York: Council on Foreign Relations, 1988) treats Gush Emunim. An insightful analysis of Menachem Begin's political doctrine, rise to power and conduct as prime minister is Sasson Sofer, *Begin: An Anatomy of Leadership* (Oxford: Basil Blackwell, 1998). Colin Schindler, *Israel, Likud, and the Zionist Dream* (London: Tauris, 1995) discusses Likud's approach to Zionism more generally.

Controversies over the proper role of religion in Israel's public life are the subject of Asher Cohen and Bernard Susser, *Israel and the Politics of Jewish Identity* (Baltimore: Johns Hopkins University Press, 2000). The classic work by Charles Liebman and Eliezer Don-Yehiya, *Civil Religion in Israel* (Berkeley: University of California Press, 1983) is still useful for background understanding, but much has changed since its appearance. On 'post-Zionism', see Laurence J. Silberstein, *The Postzionism Debates* (New York: Routledge, 1999). Two impassioned responses to the post-Zionist challenge – both part analysis, part screed, one by an American Jewish historian, the other by a philosopher educated in the United States who immigrated to Israel in 1986 – are

Jerold S. Auerbach, *Are We One? Jewish Identity in the United States and Israel* (New Brunswick: Rutgers University Press, 2001) and Yoram Hazony, *The Jewish State: The Struggle for Israel's Soul* (New York: Basic Books, 2000). Both see the settler movement as the authentic voice of Zionism. A work more reflective of the Israeli Zionist mainstream is Amnon Rubinstein, *From Herzl to Rabin: The Changing Image of Zionism* (New York: Holmes and Meier, 2000).

References

Allon, Yigal (1970) *The Making of Israel's Army*. London: Vallentine Mitchell.

'American Jews and Israel: A Symposium' (1988) *Commentary*, February: 21–75.

Ben Gurion, David (1969) *Medinat Yisra'el haMehudeshet* [The Restored State of Israel]. Tel Aviv: Am Oved.

Ben Gurion, David (1974) *MiMa'amad leAm* [From Class to Nation]. Tel Aviv: Am Oved.

Ben Gurion, David (1980) *Yihud veYe'ud: Devarim al bithon Yisra'el* [Uniqueness and Destiny: Remarks on Israel's Security]. Third Edition. Tel Aviv: Ma'arachot.

de Haas, Jacob (1927) *Theodor Herzl: A Biographical Study*. 2 vols. Chicago: Leonard.

Eban, Abba (1957) *Voice of Israel*. New York: Horizon Press.

Eban, Abba (1977) *An Autobiography*. New York: Random House.

Engel, David (1996) *Bein shihrur liVerihah* [Between Liberation and Flight]. Tel Aviv: Am Oved.

Esco Foundation for Palestine (1947) *Palestine: A Study of Jewish, Arab, and British Policies*. 2 vols. New Haven: Yale University Press.

Galnoor, Itzhak (1995) *The Partition of Palestine: Decision Crossroads in the Zionist Movement*. Albany: State University of New York Press.

Ginzberg, Asher (1947) *Kol Kitvei Ahad Ha'am* [The Complete Works of Ahad Ha'am]. Tel Aviv: Dvir.

Goldmann, Nahum (1970) *Staatsmann ohne Staat* [Statesman without a State]. Köln: Kiepenheuer & Witsch.

Gorny, Yosef (1985) *HaShe'elah haArvit vehaBe'ayah haYehudit* [The Arab Question and the Jewish Problem]. Tel Aviv: Am Oved.

Gruenbaum, Izaak (1951) *Dor beMivhan* [A Generation Tested]. Jerusalem: Mosad Bialik.

Halpern, Ben (1969) *The Idea of the Jewish State*. Second Edition. Cambridge, MA: Harvard University Press.

Hertzberg, Arthur (1979) *Being Jewish in America: The Modern Experience*. New York: Schocken Books.

Hertzberg, Arthur (1997) *The Zionist Idea: A Historical Analysis and Reader*. Philadelphia: Jewish Publication Society.

Herzl, Theodor (1962) *The Diaries of Theodor Herzl*, edited, translated and with an introduction by Marvin Lowenthal. New York: Grosset and Dunlap.

Kaplan, Mordecai M. (1955) *A New Zionism*. New York: Theodor Herzl Foundation.

Laqueur, Walter and Rubin, Barry (eds) (2001) *The Israel–Arab Reader: A Documentary History of the Middle East Conflict*. Sixth Revised Edition. London: Penguin Books.

Lilienblum, Moshe Leib (1970) *Ketavim Otobiografiyim* [Autobiographical Writings]. 3 vols. Jerusalem: Mossad Bialik.

Lustick, Ian S. (1988) *For the Land and the Lord: Jewish Fundamentalism in Israel*. New York: Council on Foreign Relations.

Mandel, Neville (1976) *The Arabs and Zionism Before World War I*. Berkeley: University of California Press.

Marshall, Louis (1957) *Champion of Liberty: Selected Papers and Addresses*, edited by Charles Reznikoff. Philadelphia: Jewish Publication Society.

McTague, John J. (1978) 'The British Military Administration in Palestine 1917–1920'. *Journal of Palestine Studies* 7: 55–76.

Mendelsohn, Ezra (1986) *HaTenu'ah haTsiyonit bePolin: Shenot haHithavut 1915–1926* [Zionism in Poland: The Formative Years 1915–1926]. Jerusalem: HaSifriyah haTsiyonit.

Mendes-Flohr, Paul and Reinharz, Jehuda (eds) (1995) *The Jew in the Modern World: A Documentary History*. Second Edition. New York: Oxford University Press.

Pinsker, Leo (1936) *Autoemanzipation! Mahnruf an seine Stammesgenossen von einem russischen Juden*. Eighth Edition. Berlin: Jüdischer Verlag.

Podhoretz, Norman (1983) 'The State of World Jewry'. *Commentary*, December: 37–45.

Ravitzky, Aviezer (1996) *Messianism, Zionism, and Jewish Religious Radicalism*. Chicago: University of Chicago Press.

Rose, Norman (1986) *Chaim Weizmann: A Biography*. New York: Viking.

Royal Institute for International Affairs (1939) *Great Britain and Palestine 1915–1939*. Oxford: Oxford University Press.

Segev, Tom (1991) *HaMilyon haShevi'i: HaYisra'elim vehaSho'ah* [The Seventh Million: The Israelis and the Holocaust]. Tel Aviv: Keter.

Shavit, Yaacov (1977) *MeRov liMedinah* [From Majority to State]. Tel Aviv: Hadar.

Sheleg, Yair (2001) 'Yehudei haTefutsot doreshim zechut hachra'ah biShe'elat har haBayit' [Diaspora Jews demand the Right to Decide the Question of the Temple Mount], *Hadoar*, 5 January: 3–4.

Shemesh, Moshe (2003) 'Did Shuqayri Call for "Throwing Jews into the Sea"?' *Israel Studies* 8: 70–81.

Smolenskin, Perez (1925) *Ma'amarim* [Writings]. 3 vols. Jerusalem: Keren Smolensky.

Sykes, Christopher (1965) *Cross Roads to Israel: Palestine from Balfour to Bevin*. London: Collins.

Tartakower, Arieh (1957) *HaHevrah haYehudit* [Jewish Society].
Tel Aviv: Massada.

Tessler, Mark (1994) *A History of the Israeli–Palestinian Conflict*.
Bloomington: Indiana University Press.

Townshend, Charles (1988) 'Defence of Palestine: Insurrection and
Public Security, 1936–1939'. *English Historical Review* 103: 917–49.

Tsur, Yaron (2001) *Kehilah keru'ah: Yehudei Maroko vehaLe'umiyut
1943–1954* [A Torn Community: The Jews of Morocco and Nationalism,
1943–1954]. Tel Aviv: Am Oved.

Vital, David (1975) *The Origins of Zionism*. Oxford: Oxford University
Press.

Vital, David (1982) *Zionism: The Formative Years*. Oxford: Oxford
University Press.

Vital, David (1987) *Zionism: The Crucial Phase*. Oxford: Oxford
University Press.

Waldman, Morris D. (1953) *Nor By Power*. New York: International
Universities Press.

Wasserstein, Bernard (1976) 'Herbert Samuel and the Palestine
Problem'. *English Historical Review* 91: 753–75.

Weizmann, Chaim (1937) *Devarim: Ne'umim, ma'amarim uMichtavim*
[Speeches, Writings, Letters]. 4 vols. Tel Aviv: Mizpeh.

Weizmann, Chaim (1966) *Trial and Error*. New York: Schocken Books.

Wisse, Ruth R. (1978) 'The Anxious American Jew'. *Commentary*,
September: 47–50.

Index